MESSAGE From the President

Welcome to Western Iowa Tech Community College! We are glad you have chosen to be a part of the Western Iowa Tech family and we are committed to helping you achieve your academic and career goals. These are exciting times at the College and we hope you will avail yourself of all the opportunities being offered.

Improvements to facilities and infrastructure are ensuring that WIT and its students keep pace in a technology driven world. One shining example is our new policy of providing each credit student, who incurs standard tuition and fees, a MacBook Air laptop loaded with curriculum-specific software. Details of the laptop distribution will be explained during orientation.

Other great features of your WITCC college environment include:

- Plenty of student activities with more than 50 clubs and organizations
- Coaching in all subjects by trained counselors and/or peers
- International travel opportunities
- Career guidance, resume building, placement assistance
- Intramural teams in a wide range of sports
- Service learning and internships
- State-of-the-art residence halls
- Fitness center facilities and programs

You will be surrounded by highly motivated learners from a variety of backgrounds... 57 counties in Iowa, 37 states and 26 countries. Talented faculty will be at your disposal to cultivate excellence and facilitate your success. A broad choice of degree programs await your selection.

Whatever your interests, goals, and ambitions, Western Iowa Tech has much to offer. Get Going!!!

Terry A. Murrell, Ph.D.
President

Advisors/Career Navigators

Sioux City Campus:

Kristy Bowman
Kristy.Bowman@witcc.edu
(712) 274-8733 x3223
Room A300

Colleen Clifford
Colleen.Clifford@witcc.edu
(712) 274-8733 x1479
Room A300

Jennifer Conley
Jennifer.Conley@witcc.edu
(712) 274-8733 x3225
Room A300

Fran DeJong
Fran.DeJong@witcc.edu
(712) 274-8733 x4213
Room A300

Pamela Ives
Pamela.Ives@witcc.edu
(712) 274-8733 x1313
Room A300

Vicky Meza
Vicky.Meza@witcc.edu
(712) 274-8733 x1478
Room A300

Nancy McMahon
Nancy.McMahon@witcc.edu
(712) 274-8733 x1331
Room A300

Karina Pedroza
Karina.Pedroza@witcc.edu
(712) 274-8733 x4208
Room A300

Amber Seppala
Amber.Seppala@witcc.edu
(712) 274-8733 x4224
Room A300

Luke Vanderzyden
Luke.Vanderzyden@witcc.edu
(712) 274-8733 x4229
Room A300

Cherokee Campus:
Wendy Ivarson
Wendy.Ivarson@witcc.edu
(712) 274-8733 x2416

Denison Campus:
Sara Klatt
Sara.Klatt@witcc.edu
(712) 274-8733 x2636

INFO REFERENCES

WEBSITES

Bank Mobile
http://www.bankmobilevibe.com
http://www.refundselection.com

Bookstore
http://bookstore.witcc.edu

Career Interest Planning
https://witcc.emsicareercoach.com

Counseling Services
www.witcc.edu/student_services/counseling.cfm

Disability Services
www.witcc.edu/student_services/disabilities.cfm

Fast Web's Free Scholarship Search
http://www.fastweb.com

Federal Financial Aid Application
www.fafsa.ed.gov

Financial Aid
www.witcc.edu/financial_aid

Meet Your New Career
www.meetyournewcareer.com

MyWIT Student Portal
https://my.witcc.edu

Scholarship Information
www.witcc.edu/financial_aid/scholarship_app.cfm

Student Activities
https://my.witcc.edu (click on "Student Activities")

Tutoring Center
https://my.witcc.edu (click on "Tutoring")

Veterans Services
www.witcc.edu/veterans/

PHONE NUMBERS

Sioux City Main Campus	712-274-6400
Denison Main Campus	712-263-3419
Cherokee Main Campus	712-225-0238
Mapleton Center	712-882-2401
Bookstore	712-274-8733, ext. 1417
Campus Emergency	712-274-8733, ext. 1316
Cashier	712-274-8733, ext. 1210
Dr. Robert E. Dunker Student Center	712-222-4477
Housing	712-274-6417
IT/Help Desk	712-274-8733, ext. 1461
Library	712-274-8733, ext. 1239
Registration Info	712-274-6404
Security—Campus Emergency	712-274-8733, ext. 1316
Security—General Inquiry	712-274-6414
Student Financial Services	712-274-6402
Testing Center	712-274-6443
Tutoring	712-274-8733, ext. 1334

2017-2018 Calendar

FALL SEMESTER 2017

Aug. 20	Housing Move-In, 1–5pm
Aug. 21 & 22	Housing Move-In
Aug. 21	Online Classes Begin
Aug. 23	On-Campus Classes Begin—on-campus & online (16 & 1st 8 week term)
Sept. 11-15	Welcome Week
Sept. 4	Labor Day Holiday; College Closed
Sept. 15	WITStock
Sept. 18	Online Classes Begin (12 week)
Sept. 20	Health Fair
Sept. 21	Club Fair
Oct. 1–31	Apply Online for December Graduation (MyWIT)
Oct. 9-13	Degree Completion Evaluation Week (for December Graduates)
Oct. 10	Transfer Fair (General Studies)
Oct. 10 & 11	Transfer Fair (Nursing & BSN)
Oct. 13	Online Classes End (1st 8 weeks)
Oct. 16	Online Classes Begin (2nd 8 weeks)
Oct. 17	On-Campus 1st 8 Week Classes End
Oct. 18-20	Fall Break; No Classes; Offices Open Oct. 20; Office Closed Oct. 18 & 19
Oct. 23	On-Campus 2nd 8 Week Classes Begin
Oct. 23	Advising/Registration Opens Spring 2018 for all Students
Nov. 6-10	Degree Completion Evaluation Week (for May Graduates)
	FAFSA Assistance Week (Financial Aid)
Nov. 23 & 24	Thanksgiving Break; College Closed
Dec. 8	Online Classes End
Dec. 21	Commencement; Fall Semester Ends; No Evening Classes
Dec. 25–Jan. 2	Winter Break; College Closed

SPRING SEMESTER 2018

Dec. 22–Jan. 18	Online Winterim Classes
Jan. 3	Advising/Registration Opens for Summer 2018 for all Students
Jan. 16	Online Classes Begin (16 & 1st 8 weeks)
Jan. 17	On-Campus Classes Begin
Feb. 12	Online Classes Begin (12 week)

2017-2018 Calendar

SPRING SEMESTER 2018 CONTINUED

Mar. 1–31	Apply for Spring/Summer Graduation
Mar. 7	Transfer Fair (General Studies)
Mar. 6 & 7	Transfer Fair (Nursing & BSN)
Mar. 9	Classes End—On-Campus & Online (1st 8 weeks)
Mar. 12	Online Classes Begin (2nd 8 weeks)
Mar. 19	On-Campus Classes Begin (2nd 8 weeks)
Mar. 12-16	Spring Break; No Classes; Offices Closed March 12 & 13; Offices Open March 14–16
Mar. 19-23	Degree Completion Evaluation Week (for Spring/Summer Graduates) FAFSA Assistance Week (Financial Aid)
Mar. 30	Spring Break; Offices Closed
April 2	Advising/Registration Opens for Fall 2018 for All Students
May 4	Online Classes End
May 17	Commencement; Spring Semester Ends; No Evening Classes
May 18-20	Housing Move Out

SUMMER SEMESTER 2018

May 28	Memorial Day Holiday; College Closed
May 29	Classes Begin—On-Campus & Online
June 1–30	Apply for Summer Graduation (No Commencement Ceremony will be Held for Summer)
June 11	Online Classes Begin (2nd 8 weeks)
June 29	First-Half Summer Semester Ends On Campus
July 9	Online Classes Begin (4 weeks)
July 2–6	No Classes; Offices Closed July 4
July 9	Second-Half Summer Semester Begins On Campus
July 23	1st 8 Week Online Term Ends
Aug. 5	2nd 8 week & 4 Week Online Ends
Aug. 9	Summer Semester Ends; No Evening Classes

NOTES: College holidays and break periods begin with the close of regularly scheduled classes on the class day immediately preceding the holiday or break period. Classes resume at their regularly scheduled starting time on the first day following a holiday or break.

The Iowa Community College Online Consortium (ICCOC) sets the online class schedule. The online semester always vary from the on campus semester by a few days.

800.352.4649 or www.witcc.edu   •   Western Iowa Tech Community College

ENROLLMENT TIPS

NOTE THE START AND END DATE FOR CLASSES:
Not all classes start and end at the same time.

ADDING A CLASS
Students may add a class through the first scheduled class day. After the first day of class, instructor approval will be required. Instructors can approve adding you to their class by e-mail to registration, registering you via the faculty registration system, or by signing an Add/Drop Form presented by you. The Add/Drop Form is available in Admissions and Advising.

DROPPING OR WITHDRAWING FROM A CLASS
The last day to drop a course or withdraw from a class is seven (7) calendar days before the last scheduled class session.

Dropping a class does not automatically mean a refund will be issued. See Refund Policies for each semester using the following links:

- http://www.witcc.edu/pdf/ImportantInfo-Fall.pdf
- http://www.witcc.edu/pdf/ImportantInfo-Spring.pdf
- http://www.witcc.edu/pdf/ImportantInfo-Summer.pdf

Students with financial aid should contact the Financial Aid Office to determine the impact on aid eligibility.

You may drop in the following ways:

- Online using the "Student Planning" at my.witcc.edu on the MyWIT "Students" tab (only before first day of class)

- By email: info@witcc.edu (include your Name, Student ID, Phone and the Course Name)

- By telephone: 712-274-6404

- In person in Admissions and Advising

Students should review their schedule to ensure the course is no longer listed on their schedule.

METHOD OF **PAYMENT**

- **PAYMENT IN FULL**
  Pay in person, by phone, or online using the student tab on **my.witcc.edu**. Pay by cash, check, or credit card.

- **PAYMENT BY FINANCIAL AID**
  Approved financial aid will be transferred to your account. Start this process early. It sometimes takes 6-8 weeks for government aid.

- **PAYMENT BY THIRD PARTY**
  If sponsored by an agency (JTP, Vocational Rehab, etc.), sign the invoice and return it to Student Accounts.

- **FACTS TUITION PAYMENT PLAN**
  Flexible monthly payment option – apply online by selecting "FACTS Payment Plan" under the student tab on **my.witcc.edu**.

AMERICANS WITH DISABILITIES ACT **(ADA)**

If you have a disability, contact **Michelle Fiechtner**, Disability Services Coordinator, at 712-274-8733, ext. 3216, for an appointment. She is available to discuss reasonable accommodations which might be of assistance to you.

MyWIT Login

MyWIT gives you access to classroom related information, grades, campus news, email, message boards and much more!

https://my.witcc.edu

NEW STUDENTS:

Login ID: Enter wit + your seven-digit student ID number. You need to enter all seven digits of your ID number including zeros
example - Login ID: wit0012345

Password: Your first initial capitalized, last initial lowercase followed by your 8 digit birthdate (mmddyyyy).
example: Jd01011980

QUESTIONS:

Contact the WITCC Helpdesk, Room A230
712-274-8733 ext.1461
helpdesk@witcc.edu

Student Email

Your student email is accessible by logging into your MyWIT account. Email is provided through Office 365 and cloud file storage is OneDrive (formerly SkyDrive).

LOGIN:

firstname.lastname@my.witcc.edu
john.doe@my.witcc.edu

PASSWORD:

Your first initial capitalized, last initial lowercase followed by your 8 digit birthdate (mmddyyyy). example: Jd01011980

QUESTIONS:

Contact the WITCC Helpdesk, Room A230
712-274-8733 ext.1461
helpdesk@witcc.edu

MyAccount FAQs

1. Where can I access MyAccount?
The MyAccount link is located on MyWIT.

2. What is MyAccount?
MyAccount is a quick, easy way to view your student account and make payments.

3. Can I pay my bill online with MyAccount?
Yes, we now offer an easy to use online payment option with no service fees. Click the tab Make A Payment to get started.

4. How do I setup a payment plan?
Payment plans may be setup through FACTS Tuition Payment Plan. Apply online by selecting FACTS Payment Plan (MyWIT.)

5. What does a negative balance mean to me?
A credit balance (negative balance) means that your charges are less than any payments or financial aid on your account and that your account is paid in full.

6. Is my credit balance my refund?
No, not necessarily. You are viewing a snap shot of your MyAccount. Any additional transactions from the time you view your MyAccount and the processing of refunds will change your balance.

7. Can I print a statement?
Yes, click on View Statement. An Adobe PDF file will open providing a printer friendly view of your MyAccount. You can save or print this document.

8. Can I view past terms?
Yes, under Term there will be a list of any term you have attended WITCC. You may select any term displayed.

Financial Aid Checklist
FAQs

1. **Why would I have a Financial Aid Checklist?**
   If you have completed a FAFSA the Financial Aid Office may require additional documentation in order to award Federal financial aid funds.

2. **What is My Financial Aid Checklist?**
   My Financial Aid Checklist is a personalized list of required financial aid items and the current status of those items.

3. **What is my responsibility for items on the Financial Aid Checklist?**
   If you want to receive Federal financial aid funds all items on the Financial Aid Checklist must be completed.

4. **How can I see what is on my Financial Aid Checklist?**
   The *Financial Aid Checklist* link is located in MyWIT.

5. **How do I know if there are items on my checklist?**
   You will receive an email to your MyWIT email account from the Financial Aid Office informing you to view your checklist or you can click on the *Financial Aid Checklist* link on your MyWIT.

6. **How do I know what item(s) need attention on my checklist?**
   Under the "Status" column, items marked "Not Received" need to be completed and those items marked "Received" have been submitted to the Financial Aid Office.

7. **How do I know what action I need to take on the items marked "Not Received"?**
   Click on the link under the "Action" column and follow the directions to complete the required step(s).

8. **When all items are marked "Received" how will I know if my financial aid was awarded?**
   Once all items have been received, please allow 7-14 processing days for your award notification. The Financial Aid Office will send you an electronic award notification to your MyWIT email account.

BankMobile

Western Iowa Tech has partnered with BankMobile, a division of Customers Bank, to provide a process for all WITCC students to receive refunds. The process is called the WITCC BankMobile Disbursement Program.

Set up refunds: http://www.refundselection.com
Manage your refund account: http://www.bankmobilevibe.com

For more information about WITCC BankMobile Disbursements Program:

Contact Financial Aid
712-274-8733 ext. 6402
finaid@witcc.edu

WITCC Student Lingo

ON-DEMAND STUDENT SUCCESS WORKSHOPS
Academic & Career Exploration
Maximizing Your College Experience
What It Takes To Be A Successful Student
Exploring Careers & Majors
Mastering The Job Interview
Writing Effective Resumes & Cover Letters
Creating Your College Bucket List: Explore, Experience, Succeed

Reading & Writing Strategies
Pre-Writing Techniques: Planning & Idea Development
Developing A Strong Thesis Statement
Drafting Introductions, Body Paragraphs & Conclusions
The Revision Process: How To Proofread & Edit Your Writing
Reading Comprehension Strategies

Learning To Learn
Discover Your Learning Style
Study Tips & Note-Taking Strategies
How To Reduce Test Anxiety
Understanding & Avoiding Plagiarism
Learning Strategies Every Student Should Know
Exam Preparation Tips & Test-Taking Strategies
How To Overcome Math Anxiety
How To Succeed In Math
10 Habits Of Mind For College Success
The Difference Between High School & College
Information Literacy: How To Master College Research
Academic Integrity: The Do's and Dont's

Personal Management
Time Management: Strategies For Success
Overcoming Procrastination: Causes & Cures
Financial Literacy: Smart Money Skills For College & Beyond
Stress Management Techniques
Navigating The Financial Aid Process
Improving Student-Faculty Relationships
How To Develop Your Cross-Cultural Skills
Setting & Accomplishing Realistic Goals
How To Achieve Well-Being, Balance & Success
Emotional Intelligence: The Other Key To Academic Success

Online Learning
10 Tips For Success In Your Online Course
Effectively Communicating Online
Online Courses: Staying Motivated & Disciplined
Taking Tests Online: Strategies For Success

Success Strategies
Student Veterans: How To Succeed In College
Success Strategies For First Generation Students
Leading As A Student-Athlete In & Out Of The Classroom

HELP WHEN YOU NEED IT – 24/7
www.studentlingo.com/witcc

QUESTIONS:
Contact Admissions
712-274-6404
info@witcc.edu

TITLE IX

TITLE IX AWARENESS & DISCLOSURE INFORMATION

Gender Discrimination, Harassment, & Sexual Violence

Western Iowa Tech Community College is committed to creating and maintaining an educational environment and workplace that is free from discrimination.

TITLE IX AND SEXUAL VIOLENCE

Title IX of the U.S. Department of Education Amendments of 1972 prohibits discrimination based on sex in education programs and activities that receive federal assistance. Examples of the types of discrimination that are prohibited under Title IX include sexual harassment, sexual assault/sexual violence, discrimination based on pregnancy and the failure to provide equal opportunity in athletics. The Violence Against Women Act (VAWA) provides protections to individuals who are the target of sexual violence, domestic/dating violence and stalking.

TITLE IX POLICY

It is the policy of Western Iowa Tech Community College, in keeping with efforts to establish an environment in which the dignity and worth of all members of the college-wide community are respected, that sexual harassment/sexual violence of students and employees at Western Iowa Tech Community College is unacceptable conduct and will not be tolerated. Sexual harassment/sexual violence may involve the behavior of a person of either gender against a person of the opposite or same gender, when that behavior falls within the following Definition.

DEFINITION

Sexual harassment/sexual violence of employees and students at Western Iowa Tech Community College is defined as any unwelcome sexual advances, requests for sexual favors, or other verbal or physical conduct of sexual nature when:

- Submission to such conduct is made either explicitly or implicitly a term or condition of an individual's academic evaluation or employment.

- Submission to or rejection of such conduct is used as the basis for academic decisions or employment effecting that individual.

- Acts of domestic violence, dating violence, and/or stalking.

- Such conduct has the purpose of or effect of unreasonably interfering with an individual's educational experience or work performance or creates an intimidating, hostile, or offensive education or work environment.

EXAMPLES

Verbal: sexual innuendo, suggestive comments, insults, threats, jokes or derogatory comments based on gender; sexual propositions or advances; pressure for sexual favors.

Nonverbal: posting of sexually suggestive or derogatory pictures, cartoons or drawings; making suggestive or insulting noises, leering, whistling, or making obscene gestures.

Physical: touching, pinching, squeezing, patting, brushing against body; impeding or blocking normal work or movement; coercing sexual intercourse; stalking or assault.

WHAT YOU SHOULD KNOW

Complaint Procedures

Persons who feel that they have been a victim of sexual violence under this Definition and wish further information or assistance in filing a complaint, should contact the Human Resources Office/Title IX Coordinator, Dean, or Supervisor. All complaints will be investigated promptly, impartially, and confidentially. Upon completion of the investigation, parties will be notified of the finding in writing.

No student or employee will suffer retaliation for reporting alleged instances of sexual harassment at Western Iowa Tech Community College.

Sexual Abuse/Violence

Western Iowa Tech Community College will not tolerate the sexual abuse/violence of students, faculty, and/or staff at any of its campuses, facilities, and/or activities. It is the policy at Western Iowa Tech to provide education to help prevent, facilitate the reporting of and provide information on counseling concerning sexual abuse.

TITLE IX

BYSTANDER INTERVENTION

1. Recognize there is a problem
2. Act and address the situation
3. Call a friend, call Security, or call the police
4. Exit the party, the room, or area

PRIVACY

Information received by the Human Resources Office/Title IX Coordinator in connection with the filing, investigation, and resolution of allegations will be treated as private. The Title IX Coordinator will disclose your information on a limited basis and only as needed to properly and thoroughly conduct an investigation, for the purposes of addressing conduct or practices that are in violation of the policy, or when required to do so by state or federal laws.

WHERE TO GO FOR HELP

Counseling, resources, and referral and advocacy services are available for any member of Western Iowa Tech student body, staff, or faculty, who believes he/she has been the victim of sexual violence. Some of the services are:

Council on Sexual Assault and Domestic Violence (CSADV)

- 712-258-7233 or 800-982-7233
- Sioux City, Iowa

Centers Against Abuse & Sexual Assault (CAASA)

- 712-277-0131 or 800-982-7233
- Sioux City, Iowa

National Sexual Assault Hotline

- 800-656-4747

Iowa Sexual Abuse Hotline

- 800-284-7821

Iowa Domestic Violence Hotline

- 800-942-0333
- For Iowa, Nebraska and South Dakota

REPORTING A COMPLAINT

Who should report?

Report if you:

- Are the victim
- Witnessed someone being a victim
- Are aware of information that someone is or might be a victim

If you are a student and report your concern to any College employee, most employees (except counselors) have a responsibility to inform the Title IX Coordinator that an incident has occurred, even if you choose to remain anonymous.

If you are an employee and report to a supervisor, your supervisor is required to report the information to the Title IX Coordinator.

The Title IX Coordinator is responsible for investigating complaints of sexual misconduct, for monitoring the response of other campus offices involved in sexual misconduct complaints, and for responding to complaints of retaliation connected to the reporting or filing of a complaint.

In order to take appropriate corrective action, the College must be made aware of misconduct or related retaliation. Therefore, anyone who believes he/she has experienced or witnessed sexual misconduct or related retaliation should promptly report such behavior to the Human Resources Office/Title IX Coordinator

REPORT ALL COMPLAINTS TO

Title IX Coordinator: Brenda Bradley
Dean of Quality and Human Resources
Dr. Robert H. Kiser Building
Human Resources Office, Room A242

Western Iowa Tech Community College
4647 Stone Avenue
Sioux City, Iowa 51106

Telephone
712-274-6400 ext. 1220

Fax (Confidential)
712-274-6471

Email
brenda.bradley@witcc.edu

Life During Community College
Your Guide to Success
First Edition

By Tawnya L. Beermann, Terry J. Arndt & Kirrin R. Coleman

COLLEGE
TRANSITION
PUBLISHING
EST. 1999

Copyright Information

Book Disclaimer

About the Authors

Tawnya L. Beermann
Tawnya Beermann earned her Master of Arts in Educational Psychology & Counseling from the University of South Dakota. She was an ASPIRE Region TRIO Achiever Award recipient in 2003. She has nearly two decades of leadership experience in the Student Services arena. She is the Associate Dean of Students & Completion Services at Western Iowa Tech Community College.

Terry J. Arndt
Terry earned his Master of Business from the University of Florida. During his education, he found that sharing information with his classmates on how to achieve financial, career and academic success was extremely rewarding. As a result of his passion for helping others, Terry developed and launched College Transition Publishing during his MBA program. Since 1999, Terry has authored and published 15 publications, written numerous papers, and presented on hundreds of college campuses to tens of thousands of college students about achieving success during the college transition process. Terry is currently the President of College Transition Publishing (www.CollegeTransitionPublishing.com).

Kirrin R. Coleman
Kirrin has a Master of Arts in Education from Wake Forest University. She is a National Board Certified teacher who teaches English on Bainbridge Island, Washington. She is the coauthor and editor of *Life During College, Life During College-The Veteran's Guide to Success, Life During Community College, Life During College-The Online Learner's Guide to Success, Life After Graduation, Backpack to Briefcase*, and *Camo to Career*.

Acknowledgments

Attending community college is an exciting and formative step for students. It is also a process with many complex parts. To create a resource that accurately speaks to community college students and that provides comprehensive support for their unique needs requires the assistance of many talented individuals. The authors would like to acknowledge and thank the following reviewers and contributors for their insightful suggestions regarding the development of this work.

1SG Doug R. Pfeffer, USA (Ret)
Executive Director
Rainier Therapeutic Riding
Gig Harbor, WA

Denny Powers
Director of Veteran Services
Coastal Carolina University
Conway, SC

Kassy Scarcia
Undergraduate Academic
Advisor – Economics
University of Maryland,
College Park
College Park, MD

Kelly Sonnanstine
Coordinator of New
Student Orientation
Richland College
Dallas, TX

Linda Taylor
Director, Student Support Services
Murray State College
Tishomingo, OK

Christopher Tipton
Director, Veteran Initiatives
University of Maryland University
College
Largo, MD

Kara Tripician, M.A.
Senior Academic Advisor
and Instructor, Psychology and
First Year Experience Courses
Aims Community College
Loveland, CO

Stephanie E. Williams
Instructional Designer,
Virtual Campus
Cochise College
Sierra Vista, AZ

The authors would also like to acknowledge **Dr. Nicholas J. Osborne**, Interim Director at the Center for Wounded Veterans in Higher Education at the University of Illinois at Urbana-Champaign, for his invaluable input and use of his content in the development of Chapter 13.

Jump Start Your College Experience

Right Now ✔

- ☐ Locate key resources such as the Tutoring Center, Career Center, Library, Counseling Services, and any others that fit your specific needs (Chapter 2).

- ☐ Manage your time wisely. Check out the latest apps listed in Chapter 17 to stay on top of your daily, weekly, and semester schedule.

- ☐ Ensure you are off to a strong start! Read "Pitfalls to Look Out For" in Chapter 1.

Your First Week ✔

- ☐ Get connected! Attend new student activities, introduce yourself to classmates and instructors, and look for student clubs to join (Developing Relationships, Chapter 5).

- ☐ Know what to expect this term by reviewing the course syllabus for each class.

- ☐ Attend class regularly and on time.

- ☐ Create a study plan and stick to it (Chapter 18, Communication, Note Taking, and Study Skills).

- ☐ Set some goals! 3 goals for today, 3 goals for this week, and 3 goals for this month. Post the goals where you can see them. Read "Five Steps to Setting Goals" in Chapter 7.

- ☐ Make your health a priority. Review "Healthy Living Exercises" in Chapter 8, Health Insurance and Healthy Living.

Table of Contents

The Lay of the Land

You, the College Student

Your Academic Success Toolbox

Your Money

Planning for Your Next Steps

Sources

The Community College Experience

Congratulations! You've made a smart choice. The fact that you're reading this book means you're at a point in your life where you've decided you're ready to begin the work of earning a college-level credential (certificate, diploma, or degree) in preparation to enter the workforce or transfer on to a four-year college or university. More importantly, you've decided to challenge yourself and expand your horizons. This book will be your guide to making the most of your community college experience.

Your choice to attend a community college may have been driven by cost, location, career field, schedule needs, or any number of factors. Community colleges are known for their versatility and can meet the needs of nearly every student, which is great news for you! Regardless of the reasons you're here, what you gain along this journey is entirely up to you.

This chapter will discuss the following topics:

- Envisioning your future

- Getting involved

- Leveraging your experiences

- Pitfalls to look out for

Envisioning Your Future

In order to successfully navigate your journey, it's best if you have a pretty good idea of where you are headed. Where do you see yourself in the next 2-5 years? How do you want to spend your time? What is your ultimate career goal? The quicker you can figure that out, the quicker you can get down to the business of building your skills and checking off the list of requirements toward meeting your goal. Switching majors multiple times can be costly and really add to the time it takes to graduate. If you haven't already set your sights on a specific career goal, you'll want to find out what career services are offered on your campus.

Visit the career center

Your campus career center is much more than a place to research post-graduation job opportunities, build resumés, and prepare for interviews. In fact, it's a great idea to visit the career center early in your first year to let them help you confirm your academic program choice, and make plans for your future career. It's also typically the go-to place to find out about internships, events, workshops, and employer information sessions.

Take a career interest inventory

Visit www.mynextmove.org and take the O*NET Interest Profiler. This tool can help you identify your interests and explore related careers. You can also search for careers based on the amount of preparation needed.

Research high demand careers

Visit www.ONETonline.org to explore new and emerging career fields and also to see a list of in-demand occupations. When you earn a credential in a high demand field, you'll be in demand—and will have great job prospects upon graduation.

Look for job shadowing opportunities

Job shadowing is invaluable for learning how people in your prospective profession spend their days. For example, if you are considering a career as a Physical Therapy Assistant, you might want to visit a few physical therapy centers and inquire about job shadowing opportunities. You might find the career of your dreams—or realize that the career you were interested in is not, in fact, the right fit for you. It's better to find out early on, so that you can focus your energy on a major that will lead to a job that truly fits your interests. Note: The Career Center can help you coordinate a job shadow.

Decide on a major (career pathway)

Career Pathways is a nationwide initiative to support developing pathways to in-demand jobs. Community colleges, regional employers, and state and federal organizations work together to map out a way for individuals to get the training and education they need to succeed in the jobs employers need to fill.

The community college offers a variety of career pathway credentials or majors you can work toward completing. Many times the credentials are "stackable," meaning you might earn several types of credentials that build upon the final credential awarded. Knowing your career goal will help you to determine which credential(s) you'll want to earn. The following description of credentials is a good overview, but you'll also want to check with your college for its official requirements.

Career Pathways

"A series of connected education and training programs and support services that enable individuals to get jobs in specific industries, and to advance over time to successively higher levels of education and work in that industry. Each step on a career pathway is designed to prepare the participant for the next level of work and education." **– Workforce Strategy Center**

1. Certificate

This is a short-term credential that can be earned by successfully completing a relatively small number of credits. Some certificates are considered non-credit, continuing education, and may not apply toward the requirements of other credentials. Most certificates are not eligible for federal financial aid. So, having a plan to pay for the coursework is very important. Some certificates are "stackable" and can be applied toward the requirements of a degree.

2. Diploma

A diploma is typically two or more full-time semesters of credit courses. Diplomas are typically eligible for federal financial aid. Some diplomas are "stackable" and can be applied toward the requirements of an Associate degree.

3. Associate degree

There are several types of associate degrees, and they typically take two years to complete, if you attend school full time. Some are designed to transfer to four-year college or university, and others are designed to allow you to hit the ground running and land a job in your chosen occupational field.

Associate of Arts degree is typically the credential of choice if you are planning to transfer to a four-year college or university to earn a Bachelor of Arts degree. Most courses in this degree plan will readily transfer to a four-year college, and be counted toward bachelor's degree requirements.

Associate of Science degree is typically the credential of choice if you are planning to transfer to a four-year college or university to earn a Bachelor of Science degree. Most courses in this degree plan will readily transfer to a four-year college, and count toward the bachelor's degree requirements.

Associate of Applied Science degree is typically the credential of choice for a student who is interested in learning a technical trade without the intention of going on to a four-year college or university. This degree is designed specifically to allow the graduate to begin working in the associated career field immediately upon completion of the degree. Courses in this degree plan generally do not transfer to a four-year college or university. However, depending upon the career field, there are some colleges that may apply these courses toward the requirements of a bachelor's degree. Not every career field requires a bachelor's degree, and some Associate of Applied Science graduates have higher earning potential than those who earn a bachelor's degree. It all depends on the industry you'll be working in.

What if I just don't know

Still having a tough time deciding on a career goal? Make regular appointments with an academic advisor, who can help you sort out all of the fine print and narrow your focus. As a community college student, you have a wide variety of academic programs to choose from that could open doors to a career that fits you. Your academic advisor can provide detailed information about academic programs, set up tours, and connect you with program faculty who can answer questions about specific programs and share insight on future employment opportunities for their specific programs. Make it a top priority to select a program that fits you. Doing so will help to ensure you are taking the proper courses and are on the most efficient path toward completion of your goals.

Get Involved

It is important to get involved both in and out of the classroom. In class, you'll want to be an active learner by listening, joining in on discussions, sharing your experiences, and participating in group learning opportunities. Outside the classroom, it is a great idea to attend events, join a club, volunteer, and use campus resources. While you're doing all of these things, you'll be amazed by the value of the connections you make. No matter what your background is, you'll find people who have something valuable to share. Others will also benefit from what you have to share. You might even find opportunities to be a leader or a mentor to other students.

College is much more than going to class and doing homework. Seek out opportunities to get involved and pursue your interests. Studies show that students who get involved in campus activities outside of class are more likely to persist and graduate. Consider volunteering, participating in clubs, serving as a tutor, applying for a work-study position, or participating in study groups. Find other students who share similar interests. Making these connections will help you settle in and feel at home with your surroundings. In the process, you'll learn more about yourself and contribute to a greater campus community.

Leverage Your Experiences

Community college students are diverse. Whether you are sitting in class, attending an event, or walking down the halls, you'll likely notice the diverse company you're in. You will have opportunities to connect with and learn from your peers during the journey ahead. Take pride in your background and the experiences you bring to the table. Perhaps you embrace innovative ideas or visions for the future, have a unique hobby, come from a different culture, or have years of career experience under your belt. No matter the combination of experiences you bring with you, you'll benefit from discussions with others who have an entirely different set of experiences to share. This is valuable experience that cannot be replicated by reading a chapter in a book.

Pitfalls to Look Out For

Unfortunately, not all students who begin working toward a college credential will persist and continue their studies through to graduation. Life happens and obstacles arise, regardless of how prepared students may be. How you respond to challenges and barriers highly impacts your chances for success. Here are some common pitfalls that can get in the way of community college success:

Not asking questions

Starting a new chapter in life and embarking on the community college experience can be a little scary and overwhelming. It is important to take a deep breath and realize that you're not alone. Each semester a new group of students starts on the very same journey. They have many of the same questions and concerns that might be running through your mind. So, don't be afraid to seek out help in answering the questions you may have. Make it a practice to ask questions on a regular basis. It can be catching. Once others see that you have similar questions, they'll open up and ask questions too. You'll be learning together and opening lines of communication with other new students. It is also important that you make it a priority to review information from orientations, the student portal, college catalog, and student handbook. Chances are, you'll find much of the information you are wondering about. You'll also discover helpful information you may have been unaware of.

Too much too soon

As a new college student, you'll find your focus and energy pulled in many directions by competing areas of interest. Keeping your academic success high on your priority list can be a challenge. Community college students often juggle busy lives off campus in addition to their academics and on-campus activities. It is important to start your college journey at a pace that reasonably fits for you. You want to balnce your time carefully and focus to ensure that you get the most out of your classes while successfully balancing other areas of your life. You might consider scaling back on your course load if you are working a full-time job, raising a family, or have other responsibilities vying for your time. You'll need to weigh your priorities and determine how your time is best invested. Pay special attention to time management tips offered later in this book.

Missing class or arriving late

Research has shown that attendance is the most important factor related to successful course completion. In fact, one study calculated the cost of each missed class leads to a .06 reduction in G.P.A. If you're not present in class, you can't possibly benefit from all the learning and interactions taking place between the instructor and students. This learning experience cannot be replicated by reviewing lecture slides or borrowed class notes.

Doing only the minimum

If you put forth only the minimum effort, you'll get only minimal results. Be sure to challenge yourself to do your best. Don't operate from the mindset that you just want to pass the courses you take. Challenge yourself to excel in your courses. When you attend all of your classes, spend adequate time studying, turn in quality work, and seek out assistance when necessary, your chances of achieving success will be excellent. Remember the phrase, "If it is to be, it's up to me." The grades you earn will reflect your efforts.

Not using the resources that are available to you

Community colleges are known for providing excellent student support services. It's not enough to just know about these services. You need to take the initiative to reach out for help and use the services that you have access to. It is your responsibility to make your needs known and communicate with the student support staff. Some common services available are tutoring, a campus counseling center, disability services, and veteran services. These are just a few. Check your campus website, student handbook, or inquire with your advisor to find out more specifics about what's available to you.

Not reading or responding to your email

Reading and responding to emails will be essential to your success as a student. From the time you apply to your graduation, key information will be shared with you via email. Instructors, student affairs offices, instructors, and others will be communicating with you via email. Missing out on this important information can put you at a great disadvantage.

Not budgeting your money

Financial struggles are very often a major barrier to college completion. Be careful how you spend your money. You need to stretch your budget to last the entire school year. This means that you need to ensure you have enough money to cover your tuition, fees, books, and living expenses. Later in this book you'll learn more about how to determine what your spending priorities should be, and how to stick to them. It can be very easy to let down your guard and order take out too often, buy the latest frivolous technology, or splurge on other items that you think you need, all of which can quickly put you into debt. Use budgeting strategies early on to avoid difficult situations that can arise due to lack of money management.

You're Ready

It's time to put all of this advice into practice. You have what it takes to make your goals reality. To get the most out of your journey ahead, stay focused, reflect on your career goals, and make connections with your peers, faculty, future employers, or that four-year college if you're planning to transfer on. Be sure to investigate and make use of all of the campus resources available to you. Keep your workload manageable by developing a good routine and schedule. Leverage your experiences and learn from others around you. Do all of these things and not only will you reach your goal, you'll enjoy the process of getting there.

College Resources

You've applied and been granted admission to the community college of your choosing. Now the faculty and staff is open arms and smiling, inviting you to attend this or that event, suggesting you check out this or that opportunity, and even—in some smaller colleges—telling you to "Stop by my office any time!"

College is a fully supported adventure that goes beyond just academics. You now have a team to help you learn, succeed, stay healthy, meet new people, and even figure out how to pay for the whole experience. The resources available to you are astounding and this chapter will introduce you to some of them.

Note that available resources vary from college to college, and your school might have different names for some of the resources highlighted below.

General Support

Dean of Students/Student Services/Office of Student Life

The Dean of Students Office serves as the liaison between students and the faculty and administration of the college. Its purpose is to provide a variety of programs and services that support the campus community. The Dean of Students usually coordinates or oversees student activities, student government, and campus safety. This office—or its website—is a great starting place for learning more about campus life. It's also the go-to resource if you have a question and you're not sure where to direct it.

Disability Support Services

This office offers academic and other important support to students with disabilities. Disability Services staff can help determine eligibility, facilitate academic accommodations, and work with other campus entities to ensure accessibility for students with disabilities, as well as provide education about disability issues.

International Student Services

This office provides orientation services, advising and counseling, employment aid, health insurance programs, banking and financial services, immigration support, and resources for families of international students.

Parent Services

If your parents are involved in your academic life, the Office of Parent Services is where they can turn when they have a question about your college or have an issue they need help figuring out. While your college experience is fully supported, your parents may feel lost amidst the FAFSA forms, tuition bills, and college lifestyle pamphlets. Parent Services provides them with information and advice, and helps them navigate the college system.

Veterans Outreach

The Veterans Outreach Center supports veterans and their families by administering benefits, providing enrollment certification, and helping with the transition from military to college life.

Money

Bursar/Student Accounts/Business Office

This office processes and collects student tuition, room, and board fees; issues refunds; and collects and disburses financial aid. Your school may also provide similar information and self-service options through your student web portal.

Financial Aid

The Financial Aid Office assists students in overcoming financial barriers to their education. The office employs experienced financial advisors who work with students to evaluate their financial needs and obtain federal, state, and/or scholarship assistance to help fund their college education.

Student Employment/Career Resource Center

The Student Employment Center connects students seeking employment with the campus or community entities who are hiring. Here you'll find work study and non-work study jobs posted, as well as volunteer, internship, and community service opportunities.

Health and Wellness

Campus Recreation or Athletic Center

Your college probably has at least one athletic center. This is a good place to meet other students or join an intramural team. A few colleges may even provide access to added amenities such as a pool, massage clinic, climbing gym, or services like fitness evaluations and training and nutrition services.

Counseling Center

Counseling centers provide mental health care, including professional consultation, referral, therapy, academic assessment, emergency services, information and education, and support groups.

Student Health Services

Some colleges offer students access to some form of quality, affordable and accessible health care services, even if students do not have health insurance.

Common services provided by student health centers include immunizations, reduced-cost prescriptions, diagnosis and treatment of common illnesses and minor injuries, pregnancy tests and contraception, and health education outreach.

Campus Life

Campus Police
The goal of the campus police is to create an environment that keeps students safe as they learn, work, live, and play. Your college's campus police may also offer classes on public safety and provide security escorts for students traveling on campus at night.

Center for Spiritual Life/Campus Ministries
Some community colleges have a faith center on campus that will help connect you to places and people that can support your spiritual life. Whether you're looking for a place to worship, a faith-based study or discussion group, or an opportunity to serve the community, this is a good place to start.

Gender Equity Center/Civil Rights and Title IX Coordinators
Your school will have a coordinator or a staff dedicated to ensuring the school complies with federal laws regarding equal access and non-discrimination. If you have a question about your civil rights or if you have a concern about harassment or discrimination, this is the office to go to first.

Multicultural Student Services Center
This office provides information, academic resources, and support for a diverse and inclusive campus community. Many multicultural centers also coordinate diversity training and sponsor campus-wide events related to their mission.

Office of Community Service
Community services offices offer volunteer and service-learning opportunities in the greater community.

Ombudsman
An ombudsman is an independent, impartial mediator who assists faculty, staff and students with communication and problem-solving. For example, if you believe a faculty member is treating you unfairly and your attempts to resolve the conflict have not been successful, an ombudsman can help you investigate your concerns, meet with relevant parties, and reach a resolution. If your college does not have an ombudsman office, check with your Student Services office if you need problem-solving assistance.

Residence Life
Some community colleges have a Residence Life office, which maintains campus housing and dining facilities, and may also develop programs and services such as meal plans, room assignments, and roommate matching. Residence Life employs Resident Assistants (RAs) who assist student with adjusting to living on campus.

Student Activities Center/Office of Student Life

Student Activities centers plan and organize fun, social, and educational activities both on and off campus for students. Examples include guest speakers, performers, intramural sports leagues, and excursions.

Student Legal Services

Some community colleges offer some form of free or reduced-cost legal services. Common cases brought to Student Legal Services staff include tenant-landlord disputes, traffic or alcohol offenses, misdemeanor criminal cases, and consumer complaints.

Academics

Academic Advising

Academic advisors help students plan their schedules, choose their majors, map out a plan for graduation, and set goals for post-graduation. Refer to Chapter 14, Academic Planning, for an in-depth discussion of this department.

Bookstore

The college bookstore offers students all the textbooks and other materials they'll need for their classes—as well as apparel. Most bookstores also offer used books at a reduced cost and end-of-term book buy-back programs.

Information Technology (IT) Center

Your IT center helps you establish your student web portal, college email account and network storage. It may also offer computer classes and help with computer-related questions.

Computer Labs

While most students have personal computers, they might use campus computer labs for some projects, to get hands-on assistance with their technology, or for printing jobs. Computer labs are also used as instructional spaces.

Honors Program

Most colleges have an Honors program that offers more challenging academics for advanced or gifted students. Access to this program typically is limited to applicants who meet certain criteria. Those students accepted receive additional support for their rigorous academic schedule. Phi Theta Kappa (PTK) is the flagship honor society for community colleges. Many four-year colleges offer substantial scholarships to members of PTK.

Library

Every college has a central library that students can use to conduct research, find recreational reading materials, or use as a quiet place to study. Most colleges also have departmental libraries. These libraries carry a more extensive selection of materials related to the specific department's needs.

Registrar/Admissions/Student Records

This office performs a range of student services, including course scheduling, fee waivers, residency and enrollment issues, transcripts, grade reporting and billing.

Tutoring Center/Writing Lab/Math Lab

Tutoring centers and labs are a great resource—and they're often free. They are generally staffed by faculty and/or students with advanced skills who have been trained to tutor others. Some require appointments while others encourage drop-in visits.

Professional Development

Alumni Association

Alumni associations are established to develop long-term relationships with students. You don't have to be a graduate to benefit from the alumni office. In fact, many of its programs are for current students. Alumni associations promote business networking and career development opportunities, special discount programs and social events. It's also a great way to connect with graduates who are interested in sharing their experience and expertise.

Career Services

Familiarize yourself with this center early on! You'll find internship placements, resumé development assistance, interviewing and networking support, career development classes and publications, job fairs, and job boards. Also, if you are a veteran, Career Services is a go-to office for learning how to articulate your military background into civilian language while getting information on military-friendly employers and career fairs.

Online Resources

You will find all of the resources listed above—and others—online. Set aside some time to explore your school's website. Take a virtual tour of the campus and community, sign up for various electronic mailing lists or text notifications, find the central event calendar, and familiarize yourself with the course catalog and department web pages.

Community Resources

Once you've familiarized yourself with your campus, take some time to get to know the greater community if it's new to you. In fact, even if you have lived in the community for years, you might find that now is a great time to explore what it has to offer you at this new stage in your life.

Explore your transportation options—when and where do the buses or subways operate?

Locate grocery stores, banks, medical centers, and other necessary businesses.

Find possible study and meeting spaces, like libraries, parks and coffee shops.

Learn where you can access Wi-Fi and where it's free.

Look for cultural opportunities: where are the art galleries, museums, and music venues?

Check out the Chamber of Commerce to find out more about local attractions, clubs and businesses.

Depending on your interests and needs, you may also want to **research nearby churches, local support groups, crisis centers, low-cost medical and legal centers, or community organizations.**

College Resources **Exercises**

1. Which resources do you anticipate using on a regular basis your first year of college? Which resources do you anticipate relying on more heavily in your last year of college?

2. Which resources sound most interesting to you? Which offices or activities would offer you the most opportunities to challenge yourself personally, socially, and academically?

3. Find out what events and activities are coming up in the next 6 weeks and select at least three to attend.

4. If you were seeking a summer internship, where would you start your search? Create a list of all the possible campus and community resources that could help you find an ideal internship.

5. If you were concerned about a friend who seemed depressed or anxious, how might you help him or her find information or assistance? What campus and community resources would be most helpful? If you were concerned about a friend who seemed to be experiencing body image issues, how might you help him or her find information or assistance? What campus and community resources would be most helpful?

6. What opportunities are there to meet and interact with a variety of people? Brainstorm ways you can connect with people of a variety of ages, backgrounds and experiences, political and religious affiliations, interests, and areas of expertise.

7. Campus Passport. Explore the campus with a partner or two and "stamp" your passport along the way by collecting a brochure or signature from each office or by taking a photograph of you and your traveling buddies at the location. You must visit the following places, but do take time to explore other resources along the way: a) Registrar's Office, b) Student Accounts Office, c) Library, d) IT Center (or a Computer Lab), e) Tutoring Center, f)Student Health Center, g) Counseling Center, h)Bookstore, i)Athletic Center, j)Campus Police Office, k)Alumni Office, l)Career Services Center, m) Multicultural Student Center, and n)Office of the Dean of Students.

8. Become an expert on one facet of the college experience and create a presentation that will inform and entertain other new students. Choose a focus area—for example, Play, Culture, Money, or Faith—and research the variety of resources available related to that focus area. Once you've thoroughly explored your focus area on line, on campus, and in the community, create a presentation to share your knowledge with others.

Visit **www.LifeDuringCommunityCollege.com**
for more resources and exercises.

Campus Activities

A worthwhile college experience goes beyond the lecture halls and late nights at the library. Your time on campus offers you many ways to be active and engaged in the broader world around you. Campus activities play a vital part in your experience outside of the classroom.

The variety of organizations, sports groups, and other social clubs available to you is endless and appeals to every interest imaginable, from niche groups (Bocce Ball Club) to broad, nationally-based organizations (Amnesty International). Take advantage of the opportunities and don't be afraid to let your curiosity get the best of you; after all, there's no better time than now to try new things.

This chapter will discuss the following:

- Types of campus activities
- How to choose activities to participate in
- How and why to commit to your chosen activities

Types of Campus Activities

There are as many on-campus activities as there are student interests. Some are one-time or seasonal events that anybody can participate in. Check your school's event calendar or the multicultural center's event calendar to find out what's going on around campus. You'll find plays, lectures, poetry readings, film screenings, debates, celebrations, and outings that are open to anyone. Whenever possible, get out and take advantage of the opportunity to experience something new and different.

> *You can discover more about a person in an hour of play than in a year of conversation.*
> Plato, Greek philosopher

Some activities are ongoing and entail a bigger commitment. Here's an overview to get you thinking about what might interest you most:

Academic Clubs and Societies

Some Academic Clubs and Societies are highly selective or invitation-only. Most simply require that you be interested in the subject. Examples include Astronomy Club, Spanish Conversation Club, and literary societies.

Culture and Identity

Some groups are formed based on the culture or identity of their members. Latino student associations and LGBTQ organizations are two examples.

Political

College has long been synonymous with political exploration and activism. From Amnesty International and Greenpeace to College Republicans and College Democrats, you will find a host of political organizations represented on campus.

Religious

Your school might have a specific religious affiliation or it might have diverse religious affiliations represented.

Why Get Involved?

- Make friends
- Get to know college faculty and staff
- Get to know community members
- Play
- Develop skills
- Learn
- Make connections
- Build your resumé

Special-Interest Groups

These groups are based on the common interests of their members. Photography clubs, mountain biking groups, and performing arts organizations are a few examples.

Sports

From intercollegiate sports to intramural sports to on-campus teams, leagues, and tournaments, there will be no shortage of ways for you to sweat; throw, hit, and bounce things; yell, shout and laugh; wear funny equipment; and wear yourself out. Lacrosse, skiing, skydiving, basketball, archery, and even bowling appear on lists of sports activities.

Student Government

Nearly every college has a student government. You can participate as an elected officer or representative from your department, dorm, or club.

What Activities are Available?

To find out about your school's activities:

Check out your school's web page. Look for these headings: Student Life, Activities, Clubs, etc.

Ask other students about organizations that may interest you.

Visit your Student Activities Center or its website and review its list of activities.

Attend a campus activity fair. Many colleges hold regular events where representatives from student organizations share information about what they do and how to get involved.

Meet with your academic advisor to ask for her or his recommendations.

Go to a meeting. Throughout the year many student organizations will host new member meetings. Keep an eye on bulletin boards and campus publications to find these meetings.

How to Choose?

Don't. At least, don't choose yet. The best part of being a first-year college student is that there's an overwhelming, exhilarating array of possibilities. You don't have to be an expert; you just have to be interested, show up, and play or work as hard as you can. We recommend that you check out a lot of activities now and get a feel for them. Try out those clubs that revolve around things you're already passionate about, but also try out the clubs that spark your curiosity or seem out of your comfort zone. Be open to finding a new passion.

After you've explored your options, reflect on what you hope to gain from your extracurricular activities. Ask yourself:

What is my motivation? Is it to make friends, develop a new skill, relax, help others, and/or get outside?

Which activities fit my needs? Make sure you fully understand the mission, values, and requirements of the organization.

Can I fulfill the requirements of the organization? Some clubs charge dues or initiation fees, or require members to travel and/or purchase uniforms and equipment. Some organizations take attendance and require members to fulfill a certain number of hours per month. Some require members to complete a task or demonstrate a certain skill level—world language clubs may require potential members to pass an oral fluency exam, for example, and scuba diving clubs probably require their members be licensed.

Commit

When you find a group you're interested in, stay in touch and informed via social media. Most campus organizations will have an events calendar you can subscribe to or a Facebook group you can join. If you want to take your commitment to the next level, choose a group or two that you can really dedicate your time to. Commitment means **attending the meetings and events regularly, showing up on time** for activities, **being an active participant** in meetings and projects, and **providing leadership** by volunteering for roles within the organization.

Active, meaningful participation will challenge and fulfill you. Sure, you don't want to overextend yourself and spend so much time on activities that your academic work suffers. On the other hand, taking some time to pursue your passions outside the classroom and lecture hall can invigorate and enrich your college experience.

Campus Activities **Exercises**

1. Make a list of three or four extracurricular activities that interest you. What would be the benefits of getting involved in each activity? What would be the commitment level? What drawbacks, if any, would there be to getting involved in each one?

2. Choose two extracurricular events or activities to participate in this week. Afterwards, write about what you did and what you got out of each experience.

3. Which extracurricular events or activities would give you the chance to be with a diverse group of people? Select one to participate in and write about the experience (or make a presentation about your experience).

Visit **www.LifeDuringCommunityCollege.com**
for more resources and exercises.

Campus Safety and Security

CHAPTER 4

The college brochure features glossy photos of ivy-covered buildings and groups of diverse students chatting in autumnal sunlight. There are photos of young people sitting attentively in a lecture hall, or cheerfully handling pipettes, or engaging in an intense discussion with a professor. You probably won't see images of security guards and campus police. It's unlikely that the brochure will include a table of statistics of crimes committed on campus. But all the scenes of comfort and learning are made possible by your college's careful attention to security and safety.

People are fond of making a distinction between college and the "real world." However, college *is* the real world; it is your real world for the next two years or so. And while your real world includes exciting lectures and maybe even sun-dappled conversations in the quad, it also contains some dangers and requires your awareness.

Your school's role in keeping you safe is to provide campus police, well-lit walkways, education on potential risks and prevention, emergency training and drills, and to coordinate with state and local agencies to stay abreast of best practices in campus security. Your role is to use these resources and education to guide your behavior.

This chapter will provide a overview of campus safety issues, including

- drinking and drugs
- sexual assault
- burglary and robbery
- identity theft
- stalking and harrassment
- cyber safety
- general safety tips

Drinking and Drugs

Your health and safety are directly affected by your use (or non-use) of alcohol and drugs. The lower your inhibitions and more clouded your judgment the more likely you are to put yourself at risk or to put others at risk. We don't intend to be preachy in this chapter, but we must be real: the college years, especially the early college years, are a time when many people experiment with alcohol and drugs. Binge drinking, while not an exclusively college behavior, is very closely associated with the college experience.

Despite being pervasive on many college campuses, alcohol and drugs are devastating to the health and safety of college students. Much of campus crime and injury is attributable to the use and abuse of alcohol and drugs, as they negatively impact behaviors and impair judgment. Here are some statistics from the National Institute of Alcohol Abuse and Alcoholism (NIAAA) to remind you of the role these substances play in the lives of college students between the ages of 18 and 24:

- Every year nearly 600,000 students are unintentionally injured while under the influence of alcohol

- More than 97,000 students are victims of alcohol-related sexual assault or acquaintance rape

- 400,000 students had unprotected sex and more than 100,000 report being too intoxicated to know if they consented to having sex

- 1,800 students die each year from alcohol-related injuries, including car crashes

The best thing you can do to protect yourself and others is to stay sober or drink responsibly. If you are in a situation where you feel people have gotten out of control, leave. If you believe others may be at risk, contact the proper authorities. You could save someone's life.

Alcohol Poisoning Symptoms

Seek help if you notice someone exhibiting the following symptoms:

- confusion, stupor
- vomiting
- seizures
- slow or irregular breathing
- blue-ish or pale skin
- low body temperature
- unconsciousness

Note: Alcohol poisoning does not necessarily involve all of these symptoms.

Source: The Mayo Clinic
www.mayoclinic.com

Sexual Assault

We'll focus on facts and tips related to the most common type of sexual assault (a female victim and a male perpetrator), though males of course can be victims of sexual attacks. Sexual assault of all forms is widely believed to be underreported. According to a recent US Department of Justice report on sexual assault of college campuses,

- Nearly 5% of college women are assaulted in a given year

- 90% of college women who are raped know their attacker

- Most women are more concerned about "stranger danger" than the possibility of being attacked by an acquaintance, friend, ex-boyfriend, or other known person

Campus security escorts and defense training are available at most colleges. By all means take advantage of these resources—just remember the safest bet is to stick with a group of trusted friends. Friends should watch out for each other,

DO NOT accept drinks from people, or leave your cup sitting around at a party. I've seen so many people roofied!

Jamie H., Sophomore, Olympia, WA

especially at parties, to make sure no one gets out of control and acts in a threatening manner toward someone else, and that no one is left isolated and vulnerable to a bad situation.

Be particularly careful around alcohol, as it is considered the #1 date-rape drug because it lowers inhibitions. To make matters worse, some perpetrators will slip sedatives, such as Rohypnol ("Roofie"), into drinks of unsuspecting partygoers. Such drugs have an amnesiac effect, and leave victims vulnerable to attack.

Burglary and Robbery

By far the most common on-campus crime is burglary. While you don't need a special pickpocket-proof wallet or a wrist-cuff for your laptop, take reasonable precautions to protect your valuables in your dorm room and when you're out and about on campus. Also, if you have a bike, invest in a good bike lock and use it.

When you're off campus, try not to carry valuables or a lot of cash. Avoid ATMs in isolated or sketchy areas.

Most common criminal offenses on US campuses (in order):

1. Burglary
2. Motor vehicle theft
3. Aggravated assault
4. Sex offenses—forcible
5. Robbery
6. Arson

Source: US Dept. of Postsecondary Education

Identity Theft

Who are you? You might delve into the depths of this question in Philosophy or Identity Politics. But in this section we're mostly just talking about your name, your social security number, and your cash.

Identity theft is when someone steals your name and personal information for their financial gain. It can come in many forms and the effects can be devastating financially for several years. College students are particularly vulnerable to identify theft because they receive frequent credit card applications, tend to store personal information on their computers and cell phones, and infrequently reconcile their bank or credit card balances. Even if you don't have many assets right now (a microwave, ten pairs of socks, and a stack of textbooks), thieves can steal your future earnings by racking up debt in your name now.

Prevent identify theft by:

- shredding credit card applications and other documents that might contain personal information
- using a firewall on your computer
- carefully reviewing bank documents and financial aid documents
- Keeping your PINs and passwords to yourself

Stalking and Harrassment

Harassment and stalking are other problems that college-aged students encounter more frequently than other age groups. According to the United States Department of Justice, there are "seven types of harassing or unwanted behaviors consistent with stalking":

- making unwanted phone calls;
- sending unsolicited or unwanted letters or emails;
- following or spying on the victim;
- showing up at a place where they had no reason to be;
- waiting at places for the victim;
- leaving unwanted items, presents, or flowers;
- posting information or spreading rumors about the victim on the Internet, in a public place, or by word of mouth.

If you have experienced two or more of these behaviors on two or more separate occasions and if you fear for your safety, notify campus police.

Cyber Safety

Here are some things you can do right now to ensure your cyber safety:

About Cyber Safety

 Have images of you or other personal information been posted online without your consent? Go to: www.withoutmyconsent.org to see what you can do.

Protect yourself by using privacy settings, lock screens, and preventative software. Make sure that if you lose your phone or lose track of your tablet no one would be able to access the personal information it contains. You can install anti-theft software that allows you to lock your device remotely. You can also install anti-virus software to protect yourself from malware. The cost of the protective software will be well worth it if your computer, tablet, or phone is compromised.

Password-protect your laptop, other devices, and accounts. Make sure you don't share your password and make sure the password is strong. Don't trust your memory to retain anything but your pet's name and birthdate? Consider using an app like PasswordBox or LastPass to organize and protect your various passwords.

Recognize phishing. "Phishing" is an email fraud scam. If you receive an email that seems legitimate—say, from your bank or your school—and it asks you to verify an important piece of personal information, such as your social security number, do not click. Do not verify information, even if it's just verifying your email address, until you call the supposed source of the request and verify that it is indeed legitimate.

Avoid using public computers or WiFi for private communication or shopping. Public computers may have a keystroke logger that records everything you type. Insecure networks might expose you to malicious mischief or worse.

Remember that nothing's temporary online. Post and share only that information and those images that you'd feel comfortable sharing with a wide audience—because it's always possible that you'll have a wider audience than you intended. Your activity on Snapchat, WhatsApp, and Facebook is a few clicks away from being shared with the world.

Don't be a cyber criminal. Let's say you're broke. Let's say you want some new music or a free movie. Remember: it's a common crime, but a crime nonetheless. File sharing software and peer-to-peer (P2P) services make it easy to share music and movies. However, if doing so violates copyright then it would be stealing. Check out respectcopyrights.org for more information, including this reminder that they have posted: "You are not anonymous."

Other Tips and Information

Colleges are required to file crime statistics with the federal government. Go to **http://ope.ed.gov/security/** if you're curious for more information about your school.

Check around your campus and community for safety education and workshops. Attending an orientation or class will help you learn more about the resources and considerations particular to your school and its environs.

We'll end this chapter with these good general tips:

Be aware of your surroundings and the people around you. Pay attention to where your belongings are at all times.

Familiarize yourself with your campus—know where well-lighted paths, emergency phones, and campus police stations are located.

Keep your cell phone on you and store emergency numbers so you can dial them easily.

Try to avoid being alone in isolated areas of the campus, when other students are not close by.

Protect your privacy. Don't list your picture, name, and contact information where people can easily access it. Assume that information you post on social networking sites is available to the general public.

If you notice another person in danger, call 911 or campus security. Do not engage with another person who has a weapon.

Do not use ATMs after dark or in isolated places.

Don't carry a lot of cash or valuables. Cash, nice jewelry, and other valuables are easy targets for thieves.

Do not accept drinks from others, as drinks can easily be drugged.

Campus Safety **Exercises**

1. Take time right now to (1) locate your campus security office, (2) program relevant emergency numbers into your phone, (3) research transportation options to and from campus: What are the hours of service? How safe is each mode of transportation?, and (4) ask around to find out if there are areas of town to avoid at certain times of the day or night.

2. Write a list of the upcoming workshops or events focused on safety. Will you attend any of them? Why or why not?

3. Assess your social network safety. On a scale of 1 to 10, where 10 is "most personal" and 1 is "least personal," how do you rate your Instagram or other social media presence? Research social network safety and security. Come up with 5 rules for yourself based on your research. Discuss your findings with classmates.

4. Research identity theft and security. Come up with 5 rules for yourself based on your research. Discuss your findings with classmates.

Visit **www.LifeDuringCommunityCollege.com**
for more resources and exercises.

Developing Relationships

College is prime time for meeting people and making connections. You are surrounded by people from a variety of backgrounds and interests. You have instructors from all over the world, instructors with experience and research in fascinating and sometimes obscure fields. The student body and faculty are diverse, but everybody has one thing in common: You and your fellow students have chosen to attend this college and your instructors have chosen to teach at this college. You share a campus, a town, and at least some values— you all believe in the importance of education, for example. This kernel of shared interest is what makes college an *experience* instead of simply a series of classes one takes.

Your relationships with instructors and other students will in many ways define your college experience. This chapter covers the following topics:

- Developing relationships with your instructors
- Getting to know your instructor outside the classroom
- Emailing and meeting with your instructors
- Difficulties with instructors
- Developing relationships with your classmates

Developing Relationships with Your Instructors

College instructors include professors, associate or assistant professors, lecturers, adjuncts, and teaching assistants. Some may have extensive experience in their field and also in teaching, others may have little teacher training. Some may be quite casual and welcoming to students, others may be more formal. Also, you will find yourself in a variety of classroom environments. You might be in a class of 8 students or in a lecture hall with 500 students.

Keep an open mind—you might think you need hands-on experiential learning, but find that a passionate lecturer is your favorite professor. You might feel lost in a cavernous lecture hall until you make a connection with the teaching assistant assigned to your section and realize that she or he's a great teacher.

Developing a relationship with your instructor depends on him or her, the situation (the number of other students, the setting, the class time and place, etc.), and you. Here's what you can do to make positive connections with your instructors in class:

Attend class regularly and on time. Research has shown that attendance is the most important factor in student success in a course. In fact, one study calculated the cost of each missed class session to be .06 points off a student's G.P.A. If you know you will miss a class, contact your instructor and inform him or her of the situation, then make sure you get notes from a classmate.

Sit in the "teacher's T"—the front row or middle section of seats—where your instructor will notice you and where you'll be more likely to stay engaged in the lecture or discussion.

Come prepared for class. Complete the reading, homework, and the suggested but optional readings.

Participate in class discussions. An interesting class depends on interested students. Do your part to add to class discussion.

Ask questions. Pursue your curiosity and interest. Also, ask questions of other students to facilitate a dynamic class discussion.

Avoid asking certain questions, such as "Is this going to be on the exam?" and "Did I miss anything?" In general, instructors want to engage students in learning, not simply to inform students how to perform for a grade. Assume you did miss something if you missed class.

Demonstrate open-mindedness and respect for your instructor. This includes addressing him or her by the proper title and pronouncing his or her name correctly.

Avoid disruptions and negative attention. Turn off or silence your phone before entering class. Make sure your actions and body language convey interest in class. Slumping, texting, and madly scribbling in one's daily planner all communicate, "I'd rather be somewhere else, anywhere else, with someone else!" even if what you're actually texting is, "this class is amazing!" Also, if you know you'll have to leave class early, let your instructor know at the beginning of class. Finally, eat or drink in class only if you know it is acceptable with your instructor.

Getting to Know Your Instructor Outside of the Classroom

Outside of the classroom, you can create other opportunities to develop a relationship with your instructor. Take time to visit with your instructors—take advantage of their offers to assist students, and ask for help and advice when you need it. Also, try to attend any out-of-class gatherings or field trips where you'll be able to learn more about the subject you're studying and connect with instructors and classmates.

Here are some reasons you might meet with your instructor outside of class:

- To request guidance on a paper topic, research project, or other issue
- To ask him or her to point you to resources to help you succeed in class
- To learn more about your instructor's area of expertise or her or his department
- To obtain advice about how to do better on future assignments and exams
- To make contacts within an industry in order to get an internship or job
- To seek guidance on future education and career plans

If you do end up developing a strong relationship with your instructor, you may end up asking him or her to act as your mentor or your academic advisor. She or he may invite you to work as a teaching, lab, or research assistant, which will broaden and deepen your experience in the field. Also, scholarships, jobs, internships, and graduate schools almost always require letters of recommendation from applicants. You will want at least a couple of instructors to know you well and who will be willing to write you a letter of recommendation.

Emailing Your Instructors

Always, always, treat an email to an instructor with the same care you would an old-fashioned letter. That is, include an appropriate salutation (*Dear Professor _____ or Dear Dr. _____,*); proper spelling, capitalization, and punctuation; and a closing statement. While there may be some exceptions, most of the instructors we know and work with grimace at sloppy, informal emails. Also, make sure the content of your email is something you'd feel comfortable talking about in person. If you have a question about why you received a certain grade on a test, for example, use the email only to request an appointment to discuss your concern.

Use email...

To request an appointment. Include the purpose for the appointment and propose a time or two that might work: "Would you be able to meet with me on Wednesday afternoon to discuss possible paper topics?"

To request clarification on an assignment. Before you use email for this purpose, make sure you have thoroughly read the directions provided.

To inform your instructor about something. For example, you might email to say you won't be in class for a couple of days because you are ill. No need to go into detail—just give information that is relevant to him or her.

As suggested by the instructor. Some instructors prefer email communication and invite their students to discuss topics with them via email.

Never use email...

If you need an immediate response. Assume you won't get a response to an email for 24 hours.

To ask about why you got a certain grade. Email is too cumbersome for this purpose and you'll miss a good opportunity to improve as a student. Request an appointment, then bring in the paper or test so you can discuss it in person. She or he can elaborate on written comments and you can ask for ways you might improve in the future.

To complain or confront. If you feel strongly about a grade or issue, you should request an appointment and talk privately with your instructor. Face-to-face communication is much more effective for these situations: you will be more likely to come to a mutual understanding if you approach your instructor personally and with an open mind.

To include your instructor in your circle of friends. Refrain from forwarding mass emails or sending very personal messages to your instructors.

Meeting with Your Instructors

With a few exceptions, your instructors will be very busy people who try to make themselves available to students as much as possible. Here are some tips for planning to meet with your instructors:

Schedule an appointment. Even if your instructor holds regular office hours, try to schedule an appointment to ensure you get to meet with him or her during that time.

Earlier is better. Like you, your instructor will have more competing issues to deal with as her or his day progresses. To get your instructor's full attention, schedule your meetings as early in her or his daily schedule as possible.

Be on time. Locate your instructor's office prior to your scheduled appointment and make sure you get there when you're expected. This will show that you value his or her time and it will ensure that you have a full meeting. If you will be late, contact him or her right away to apologize and let the instructor know. Offer to reschedule if it is more convenient for your instructor.

Avoid transition times. The times right before and right after class are usually not a good time to ask your instructor for assistance or guidance. Those transitions are not conducive to focused one-on-one conversations, as there will be a throng of other students competing for your attention and the instructor will be focused on getting materials together for class.

Come prepared. Carefully review the materials that have been presented in class. If you're going to ask for clarification or help, make sure you've done as much as possible to help yourself prior to the meeting. Bring your textbook and notes if necessary.

Difficulties with Instructors

You may encounter communication issues or other difficulties with instructors. These can be particularly frustrating your first year when you are establishing your independence and learning how to deal with conflict on your own. Here are the most common frustrations students have with instructors and ways of dealing with them:

Frustration #1:
I don't understand the material!
Make an appointment to talk with your instructor. In the meeting, ask specific questions rather than asking for general help. (*What made Piaget's use of psychometrics revolutionary?* rather than *Why is Piaget important?* and never *Now, what's a Piaget?*) Bring materials like homework assignments or notes to show that you have attempted to learn the material on your own. Listen and take notes.

Frustration #2:
I understand the material but my grade doesn't show it!
Make an appointment to talk with your instructor. First, make sure that you do in fact understand the material by showing some of your work and explaining your understanding of key concepts. This will give your instructor a chance to confirm you know your stuff or to tell you that you aren't actually mastering it the way you thought you were. If your grades don't reflect your knowledge, ask for ideas for how to perform better on exams and papers. Usually instructors are happy to work with interested students.

Frustration #3:
My instructor and I can't communicate!
If you and your instructor have poor communication or a negative relationship, try contacting other students who have taken courses from him or her and ask for their recommendations on how to work with him or her. If one of you has offended the other, make an appointment and do your part to clear up any confusion.

Frustration #4:
I don't have difficulties with my instructor—I have a difficult instructor!
If you believe you've done everything you can to have a neutral to positive relationship with your instructor and nothing has worked, contact your academic advisor or college counselor for assistance and advice.

Developing Relationships with Your Classmates

Later in life you may have to rack your brain to think of topics of conversation when you're in a roomful of strangers.

But now you're on easy street. You can look around at the other seven or fifty-two or four hundred students and know you have countless things in common and therefore an abundance of conversation topics. The latest reading. The most recent assignment. The last lecture. The upcoming exam. A related play or performance. Other classes. Coffee—where to get it, how much you need it, and how much you'd pay to have a cup of it materialize in your hands at this very instant. You get the picture.

It's relatively easy to meet the people around you and to strike up a simple conversation. Even in large lecture halls many people end up sitting in the same sections each class period, so it's a good chance you'll run into the same students on a regular basis.

Build connections with other students during the transition times (the minutes before and after class) by engaging in conversation, asking questions, and comparing notes or ideas. Join field trips and other excursions that your instructor might offer; not only is it fun to learn outside the classroom, it's also an informal environment conducive to developing peer relationships. Finally, collaborate with other students: create a study group or join one that's already formed, work on a group project if that's an option, and share ideas.

Developing Relationships in the Online Learning Environment

Some of your classes may have an online component and some may be entirely online. Developing relationships with your online instructor or classmates will make such classes richer and more rewarding. In many cases, the instructor will facilitate community building by requiring a certain number of posts or other online interactions. If possible, go beyond the requirements: get involved in the online discussions, reach out to classmates to create teams or study groups, and share interesting ideas and information that is relevant to the class material.

Developing Relationships **Exercises**

1. What qualities does a great instructor possess? List as many as possible.

2. Think of teachers you've had in the past who were great but whose teaching style was very different from what usually works best for you. What made those teachers great?

3. What expectations do college instructors have of their students that are different from the expectations high school teachers have of their students? Brainstorm with another student and/or interview upperclassmen and/or instructors to answer this question.

4. Draw or describe in writing your vision of the ideal student-instructor-classmates relationship. Where do teaching, learning, and knowledge fit into your drawing or depiction?

5. Interview a classmate and introduce him or her to the class. Create interesting interview questions so other students will really get to know your subject. Introduce him or her in a memorable way.

Visit **www.LifeDuringCommunityCollege.com**
for more resources and exercises.

Academic Integrity

Cheating is tempting, easy, and costly. It's also on the rise, perhaps because certain websites and networks of students portray academic dishonesty as an inevitable part of college life, just another tool to use. Some students who have misgivings about cheating find themselves in situations where it seems like the only option. The costs depend on the situation, but could include zero credit in a course or expulsion from school. Of course there are other, unquantifiable consequences, such as an uneasy conscience.

In this chapter we will:

- define academic integrity and academic dishonesty
- discuss the pressures or attitudes that encourage academic dishonesty and how to handle them
- outline some of the possible consequences of academic misconduct

What is Academic Integrity?

The core value of higher education is academic integrity. The Center for Academic Integrity, a consortium of institutions based at Clemson University, defines academic integrity as "a commitment, even in the face of adversity, to five fundamental values: honesty, trust, fairness, respect, and responsibility."

Students need to trust professors to teach and evaluate honorably and fairly, and professors need to trust their students to behave and act honorably and responsibly. A college without such standards would have no purpose: The interactions between students and professors would be pointless and a degree from such an institution would be meaningless.

Administrators, instructors, and students all have a responsibility for promoting and supporting academic integrity.

What is Academic Dishonesty?

Academic dishonesty encompasses a range of misdeeds, most of which involve taking credit for work, words, or knowledge that is not yours. Cheating includes:

- Turning in an assignment completed by someone else
- Obtaining an exam or exam questions before your exam time
- Giving or receiving answers on an exam (during or before the exam itself)
- Unauthorized storing of information in any form that may assist you on an exam
- Arranging to have someone take an exam on your behalf
- Aiding another person in an unauthorized manner (e.g., taking an exam on that student's behalf, writing a paper or sections of a paper on the student's behalf, etc.)
- Using unauthorized notes, study aids, or technology
- Collaborating without prior approval (e.g., completing an assignment with another student in class)
- Fabricating data, results, or sources
- Submitting work done for one instructor to another instructor (e.g., turning in the same essay to two different instructors)
- Falsifying records (e.g., forging a signature on a prerequisite form, breaking into the computer system to change a grade)
- Robbing other students of resources (e.g., tearing pages out of an academic journal in the library, hiding a book in the stacks of the library)
- Plagiarizing a book, article, web site, or other source

While all of the examples listed above would be considered academically dishonest behavior at any school, it's a good idea to read over your school's honor code and/or academic honesty guidelines for more specific examples and information.

> **PLAGIARISM:**
>
> Copying someone's work and passing it off as if it's your original idea. Give credit to the source of each idea, paraphrase, summary, and direct quote in your work. If no author is listed on the source material, credit the organization, article title, or website.

Plagiarism

Let's go into detail on this one, as it's the source of confusion for some students. **Plagiarism is copying someone's work and pretending you wrote it** (definition from www.justice.gov). **If you paraphrase, summarize, or directly quote another work you must cite your source! Not citing a source is the same thing as claiming the ideas and words are original to you; thus, it's plagiarism.** A recent *New York Times* article on plagiarism in the digital age explored how some students consider web content free, open, and therefore something one can use without giving credit. That is a dangerous presumption: Whether the source material has one author or a thousand authors with none listed (e.g., Wikipedia), it needs to be cited.

Why do Students Cheat?

Students decide to cheat for a variety of reasons. The most common reasons are feeling overloaded, insufficiently prepared, or overwhelmed by personal issues. Other reasons include:

Environment. If the people around you consider cheating acceptable behavior, it can be easy to slip into the same mindset.

Poor pacing or preparation. Students who get behind sometimes consider cheating a means to an end. They see it as a lifesaver that will help avert an oncoming disaster. Other students feel underprepared and lack confidence in their own abilities, so they cover up their weaknesses by taking other people's work.

Pressure. Some students put enormous pressure on themselves to be successful, then feel they have to cheat in order to live up to their performance standards. Other students have pressure from parents or within their program to meet a certain grade point average.

Inability to say 'No.' Some students find it difficult to say no to friends who ask them to help cheat. They would rather avoid the awkwardness of denying a friend a favor and risk damaging their own academic credibility.

Collaboration or Cheating?

In some circumstances, collaboration is valued, promoted, and even required. In other cases, collaboration is cheating. Check with your instructor to make sure you have his or her permission before you collaborate with another student or students.

How to Maintain Your Academic Integrity

The key to maintaining your credibility and academic honesty is to be vigilant. Scrutinize your own actions. Avoid justifications, such as "This professor is too hard anyway" or "I knew the material, I just didn't have the busywork part of it done" or "The deadline is unreasonable" or "Just this once."

Always ask yourself, "Will I be proud when I look back on this?" and, "Would I do this if my professor were right here?"

Pace yourself to avoid a crisis situation where cheating seems like a good alternative. If you do procrastinate—and many of us do—turn in your own original work, even if it's poor. You can also try discussing the situation with your instructor to see if he or she would be amenable to accepting late work.

Get help when you don't understand a concept or just can't seem to master a skill. The tutoring center, the writing center, and your academic advisor should be able to help you or point you to the resources you need.

Be part of the solution. Hold yourself and others to high standards, and do your part to uphold the values of your college. Sometimes this means having an awkward conversation with a friend who has asked you to cheat. Sometimes it means informing an instructor when you know that classmates are cheating.

> *If you don't quit, and don't cheat, and don't run home when trouble arrives, you can only win.*
>
> **Shelley Long, American actress**

Because academic integrity is so highly valued, you will find that in general instructors and tutors respond very positively to students' requests for support and guidance in this area.

When a Friend or Classmate Cheats

What should you do if you suspect or know that a friend or classmate is cheating? Situations you might encounter include being asked to share exam questions and answers with somebody who hasn't yet taken the exam; learning that a friend has hired an essay writing "service"; and witnessing a classmate using unauthorized materials (such as a cell phone or notes) during an exam. There are so many potential hypothetical situations that it's impossible to give just one answer.

A student who senses a classmate peering at her desk during an exam might simply shift positions to better hide her answers. We know at least a couple of students who dealt with similar situations by pretending to mark incorrect answers correct. While that might be an extreme response, it does stem from strong feelings that students need to earn their grades, not steal them.

Here are some possible steps to take if you strongly suspect or know that a friend or classmate is cheating. Not all situations are equal, so use your judgment as well as any guidelines provided by your school.

Review your school's honor code or academic honesty policies to see if there are recommended or required procedures to follow.

Communicate directly to the student(s) who is contemplating cheating or who has already done so and express your concerns.

Inform the instructor privately. A face-to-face conversation is best, but email will do if you have no alternative.

Telling on a fellow student seems distasteful to most people. However, knowing about an incident of academic dishonesty and not doing something to prevent or reveal it makes you complicit. Deal with the situation honorably and you will be able to balance your loyalty to your classmate and your loyalty to your school.

Cheating in college is a serious offense that could result in significant consequences. In some cases, the instructor alone may reprimand a student who is caught cheating. However, many colleges require instructors to report any form of cheating to the college's administration.

Students who are accused of cheating usually are provided the opportunity to defend themselves to the department head, college administration, or even a student court. If the student is found guilty, he or she could face a variety of punishments, including failing the course, being put on suspension, or even being expelled. In addition to these punishments, the student may experience added stress, embarrassment, and loss of credibility. Additionally, in most cases, if a student is found guilty of cheating, the incident will be documented in the student's school records, which may cause considerable difficulty if the student applies to another institution to pursue an advanced degree.

Some colleges have revoked degrees after determining that students had cheated.

In some cases, degrees have been revoked well after the students have graduated. In one famous case, a physics professor at the University of Virginia was informed that many students in his introductory physics classes had cheated on their term papers. When he investigated the accusation, he found that 122 of his students from the previous five semesters had indeed plagiarized. As many as half of those students were expelled from the university and several students who had already graduated had their degrees revoked.

Academic Integrity **Exercises**

1. Obtain a copy of your college's policy on academic dishonesty. Summarize the process a student would go through if accused of cheating.

2. According to the honor code of your college and/or its policy on academic dishonesty, what are you required to do if you know another student is cheating?

3. Imagine you are taking an exam or working on a class assignment. As you write your answers, you sense that the person behind you may be cheating by looking at your answers. Describe what you would do in this situation.

4. With a partner or group, read the following paragraph and answer the questions. Be prepared to present your answers as part of a class discussion.

   Your friend, who is sitting near you during an exam, pulls out his cell phone surreptitiously and refers to it frequently as he works on his exam. It's clear to you that he is cheating.

   What do you think most people would do in this situation?

   What should you do?

   Are your answers to these questions different? If so, explain.

5. With a partner or group, read the following paragraph and answer the questions. Be prepared to present your answers as part of a class discussion.

   Although she is a dedicated student, Claire has struggled to keep her GPA above a 3.0. She needs to maintain a 3.0 or better in order to continue to qualify for a tuition scholarship. This semester she is enrolled in a class with a professor who is a notoriously hard grader. Her roommate offers her a copy of a test from last year's class with that same professor.

   What should Claire do?

   What variables in the scenario are most relevant to answering the question above? (Claire's dedication as a student? Her GPA pressure and scholarship? The professor's reputation?)

Visit **www.LifeDuringCommunityCollege.com**
for more resources and exercises.

Intelligence, ambition, and hard work can carry you far, but true success depends on other factors that aren't so measurable. Your life in general and your college experience, in particular, will be richer if you:

- maintain a positive attitude

- develop high self-esteem and self-efficacy

- set goals and make plans for attaining them

- know how to contribute to and get the most out of teamwork

- explore and celebrate the diversity around you

And, coincidentally, this chapter will cover all those topics!

Attitude

What is credited with delaying aging and has (practically) its own section in the book store? That's right: A positive attitude. It's not measured on any report card, but it's one of the most important attributes a college student can possess. Your attitude towards your classes, living situation, peers, and yourself may be even more influential to your success and happiness than your skills, talents, and knowledge. And if you don't already tend to have a positive attitude there's good news: You can learn to develop a habit of positive thinking. In this section, we'll define a positive attitude and give you tips for creating and maintaining one.

What is a Positive Attitude?

It's difficult to pinpoint just what separates those with positive attitudes from those without, but there are some traits closely associated with positive attitudes:

Optimism - Positive people tend to have hope and to see the good in a situation.

Persistence - Positive people believe problems can be resolved and puzzles can be solved. Their hope leads them to persist, to not give up.

Enthusiasm and energy - Positive people exhibit enthusiasm in day-to-day life.

Curiosity - Positive people are curious about the world and are driven by the desire to learn.

Creativity - Positive people are able to shift perspectives and consider problems and ideas from new angles.

Confidence - Positive people have high self-esteem and are confident in their abilities.

Resourcefulness - Positive people work to find a solution when they encounter a problem.

Vision - Positive people envision possibilities and see the best in things—and people.

Sense of purpose - Positive people believe they have a purpose in life and act on that assumption.

Strong relationships - Positive people cultivate good relationships with family, friends, and neighbors.

10 Steps to a Positive Attitude

Learning to create and maintain a positive attitude will help you enjoy college and get more out of it.

1. Give yourself a dose of perspective.

You got a bad grade on a test, you argued with your roommate, and your student loan check has been held up. It's difficult to be positive when things pile up like this. But putting things into perspective can keep you emotionally afloat. Try viewing your situation from another angle: What did you do right? What will you learn from the experience? How could it be worse? What will these problems look like when you reflect back on them a year from now? How about five years from now?

2. Be confident.

Believe in yourself and your abilities. For example, if you got a bad grade on a test, have confidence that you will work hard to figure out how to do better.

3. Surround yourself with positive people.

Seek out interesting, enthusiastic people. Reconsider relationships you have with people who thrive on negativity and bring you down.

4. Don't dwell.

Yes, you want to reflect on your actions, accomplishments, and mistakes. But use that self-reflection to move forward. Too much attention on the past can result in what one of our colleagues aptly calls "Analysis Paralysis."

5. Get busy.

It's hard to dwell on the negative when you are involved in activities you enjoy, like sports, clubs, or volunteering.

6. Plan.
Plan things you can look forward to and work toward.

7. Learn from mistakes.
As Winston Churchill said, "All men make mistakes, but only wise men learn from their mistakes."

8. Be flexible.
There's only so much you can control, and some of the most interesting and inspiring moments will come when you haven't planned on them.

9. Communicate positively.
You've seen the signs: "See something? Say something!" OK, in one context it's an anti-terrorism slogan. But in another context it can be an affirming reminder to celebrate the positive. See something cool? Say it's cool. Compliment, thank, and congratulate people in your life.

10. Make a commitment and follow through.
Few things are as gratifying as reaching a goal you have worked hard to achieve. Set short-term and long-term goals, commit to them, and celebrate your accomplishments.

Maintain Your Positive Attitude
Positive thinking is a habit that needs to be cultivated and supported. Different people have different requirements for maintaining a positive outlook, but we can boil the specifics down to three general tips:

> *What is the difference between an obstacle and an opportunity? Our attitude toward it. Every opportunity has a difficulty, and every difficulty has an opportunity.*
>
> **J. Sidlow Baxter**

Be nice to yourself. Everything is going to look pretty dim pretty fast if you are exhausted, starving, and stressed out. Treat yourself well: Eat healthily, get enough sleep, and pace yourself.

Be nice to others. Show interest in others by listening, asking questions, and paying attention. Express gratitude and praise when it's appropriate. Help out a friend who's struggling.

Look for good. Attend each lecture or activity with an eye toward the positive. Look for at least one good thing about each class period or event.

Self-Esteem and Self-Efficacy

In this section we'll talk about two factors critical to success and happiness: self-esteem and self-efficacy. Don't worry, we won't suggest you paste up sticky-notes with happy messages to yourself all over your apartment. If you want to do that, great, but our mission here is simply to define self-esteem and self-efficacy, discuss their importance in one's life in college and beyond, and provide tips for developing them.

Self-Esteem

Self-esteem is the pride and respect one has for oneself. If you hold someone in high esteem, you value and respect them. If you hold *yourself* in high esteem, you value and respect yourself. High self-esteem is not cockiness; in fact, most people with high self-esteem do not brag or flaunt their stuff because they don't rely on extrinsic validation. People with high self-esteem tend to value and respect others.

> *It is of practical value to learn to like yourself. Since you must spend so much time with yourself you might as well get some satisfaction out of the relationship.*
>
> **Norman Vincent Peale,**
> **American author**

Self-esteem is reflected in the way you:

- talk to yourself
- think about yourself and others
- meet a challenge
- respond to criticism
- face adversity

The inner monologue reveals how a person sees him or herself. A person who dwells on his or her weaknesses and failures—and, by contrast, everyone else's strengths and successes—will tell him or herself disrespectful "truths":

By making yourself aware of your own inner monologue, you can adjust it to be kinder, more forgiving, and more celebratory.

Self-esteem also affects how you respond to criticism and setbacks. Someone with low self-esteem will perceive criticism as a direct attack or proof that his low opinion of himself is well-founded. If he experiences a setback, he will give up. By contrast, a person with high self-esteem will be much more persistent and less likely to see criticism as a personal affront.

Your self-esteem will affect your academic life, so it's a good idea to reflect on your perceptions of yourself and to make sure they will have a positive influence. The National Association for Self-Esteem has a tool on its website that allows visitors to answer a series of questions and rate their self-esteem. **www.self-esteem-nase.org**

Low Self-Esteem Statements	High Self-Esteem Statements
Everyone else is better at this than I am.	*I can do this!*
I'm worthless.	*I accept and like myself.*
I messed up again! That's just like me.	*I made a mistake.*

The Self-Esteem Workout

Here are some exercises you can do on a regular basis to bolster your self-esteem:

Don't compare. Value yourself, value others, and don't waste time measuring the differences.

Don't dwell. Move on from past mistakes and embarrassments. If you find yourself dwelling on something, get busy or get help.

Be accountable. Taking responsibility for your own actions will help you respect yourself more.

Develop diverse interests. Imagine a three-year-old at a playground. There's no "I won't go on the slide, I'm not really good at slides, I'll just stick to sitting in these wood chips"! Now imagine yourself 30 years from now: What activity or interest will you be proud of yourself for trying? Will you care if you weren't perfect at it?

Compliment others. Recognizing others for their successes is great practice for recognizing your own.

Take risks. When you take a risk and succeed you've just amped up your willingness to take another, bigger risk. When you take a risk and you fail you can congratulate yourself for being the type of person who takes risks.

Give yourself credit—and rewards. Remind yourself of your successes, talents, and good qualities.

Be grateful. Divert negative thoughts away by reflecting on the things for which you are grateful.

Take care of yourself. If you value yourself, you value your health. When you feel healthy, you're more likely to feel good about your overall well-being.

Self-Efficacy

Remember *The Little Engine That Could*? "I think I can, I think I can," he chugged all the way up the mountain. That's perceived self-efficacy, but for some reason the title *The Little Engine with Perceived Self-Efficacy* never caught on.

First, let's clear up how self-efficacy differs from our previous topic, self-esteem. Let's consider our Little Engine again. If he were to tell himself "I'm a good engine! I respect myself! I have value!" he would be expressing positive self-esteem. When he believes that he can accomplish a task ("I think I can!") he is expressing a positive perception of his capability.

Albert Bandura, the influential Stanford psychologist, defines **perceived self-efficacy** as "people's beliefs about their capabilities to produce designated levels of performance that exercise influence over events that affect their lives. Self-efficacy beliefs determine how people feel, think, motivate themselves and behave." A person with high perceived self-efficacy believes she or he is very capable of performing well and can influence her or his own life.

What is your perceived self-efficacy? Do you believe you are capable? Do you believe you have influence over your life?

It depends, right? Most of us, if challenged to grow three feet taller or to become invisible or to be the next NBA superstar by Wednesday, would have low self-efficacy. We would doubt our capabilities to accomplish those goals because they are impossible or next to impossible. We would feel frustrated or apathetic, think "I can't. No way!" We would be completely unmotivated and behave accordingly.

If, on the other hand, we were challenged to learn to snowboard, or paint with watercolors, or make a birdhouse, most of us would have significantly higher perceived self-efficacy. Some students enter college with a strong sense of their capabilities, and others need to develop theirs. In order to understand your own perception of self-efficacy, consider the influences on it:

Success and failure. If you try something and succeed, you'll be more likely to think you can do it again or do the next step in the process. Bandura terms these "mastery experiences." Think about your first time at bat in a baseball game or the first time you completed a set of fractions: how did those mastery experiences influence your next attempt? Failure can influence a person as well. When you have a strong sense of efficacy, though, you tend to see failure as temporary and it challenges you to redouble your efforts. The author J.K. Rowling, for example, received multiple rejections before a publishing house took a chance on her book, *Harry Potter and the Sorcerer's Stone.* Her persistence paid off, to say the least.

Social models. When we see people around us accomplish something it shows us that it's possible and that we can do it, too. On the other hand, if there are no models we might think something is out of reach or impossible.

Social persuasion. Other people around us give us messages about our abilities, for better and for worse. If you believe these other people they can be very influential. Think about the teacher who believed in you when you didn't. (Or the teacher who didn't believe in you.) Parents, teachers, and peers have a big impact on us—that can last well beyond our time with them.

Emotional states. Think about how difficult some tasks seem when you're overtired, or how little energy you may feel when you're sad. Our state of being influences how we interpret our performance and our perception of our own efficacy.

The above information was adapted from Albert Bandura's work. See Sources section for more information.

Developing Self-Efficacy

> *So why do I talk about the benefits of failure? Simply because failure meant a stripping away of the inessential. I stopped pretending to myself that I was anything other than what I was, and began to direct all my energy into finishing the only work that mattered to me.*
>
> **JK Rowling, British author, Harvard Commencement Address, June 2008**

Once you understand the influences on your perception of self-efficacy, possibilities open up for how to develop it. Here are some:

Set yourself up for success. Give yourself tasks where you can be successful. Break up big projects into little chunks and note your ability to tackle them.

Consider failures opportunities. A failure isn't a Stop sign; it's a Detour.

Choose your social models. Hang out with friends who inspire you and believe in you and do the same for them. Connect with instructors you admire and respect.

Recognize your emotional state. If you do poorly on a test, recognize the physiological and emotional factors that influenced your performance. Were you exhausted? Overly anxious? Depressed? Don't see your poor test score as indicative of you in general but of your performance on a given day in certain circumstances.

Goal Setting

A successful college student sets goals and makes specific plans for achieving them. This section will show you how to do just that, by discussing how to set goals, establish meaningful goals, and stay motivated.

Five Steps to Setting Goals

Here's a process for setting goals that ensures you attain them:

1. Establish a goal

First, ask yourself what you want to accomplish. Be specific. For example, if you want to improve your grades, clarify what grade you'd like to earn in each class.

2. Create an action plan

There is never just one way to accomplish a goal, but there is some way. If you want to be successful, be as specific as possible when you create your plan. If your goal is to run a marathon eight months from now, for example, your action plan should include how many miles per week you need to run, what kind of adjustments you will need to make to your diet, and what time of day will be best for your training.

3. Divide your goal into smaller achievements

Learn Mandarin Chinese! Save $10,000! Get a 4.0! Goals can be daunting sometimes. Make it less intimidating—and more achievable—by breaking it into smaller, more accessible goals. For example, if your goal is to learn a new language, you might break it into the following steps: register for an introductory class, join an evening conversation group, spend a term in a country where that language is spoken, etc.

4. Set a target date

You've seen the inspirational posters: A goal is a dream with a deadline. It's true. A person decides she'll get out of credit card debt. But when? Next month? In 40 years? What if she pays off the plastic in April and runs it up again in June? How will she know if she's achieved the goal satisfactorily? Be specific with your timeline so you can stay motivated.

5. Identify your motivators

Speaking of motivation—what's yours? The rest of these tips focus on the How, but this one is about the Why. Why do you want to get in shape? To look good? To improve your health? To perform better in your favorite sport? When you identify why you want to do something you will be better able to stay on track.

Meaningful Goals

Setting impossible goals is a sure way to frustrate yourself; setting trivial ones won't do much for you either. The key is to develop realistic, meaningful goals. Here's how:

Think short-term and long-term. Some goals are accomplished in one week; others take years. Establish both kinds for yourself so you get the satisfaction of achievement along the way to your bigger goals.

Make sure they're your goals. Your mom might want you to pursue a career in medicine, your classmates might expect you to go into law, but if your heart tells you to become a physical therapist—well, others' plans for you don't matter. Similarly, if everyone else is set on getting a high-paying job right after college and you don't hear that particular siren's call, decide what *you* want to do.

Prioritize. Sometimes goals compete for time and attention. You may want to earn a 3.6 this semester, learn to play banjo, and meet new friends. Which is most important? Which one needs to be addressed right away and which one can wait? The answers will depend on you.

Challenge yourself. Sure, you want realistic, achievable goals, but they should also stretch you. If your goals are too easy to achieve, you might become bored or not enjoy the satisfaction of accomplishing them.

Be flexible. Things change and you may need to adjust a goal or replace it with another one, or you might need to alter the action plan and find a new way to achieve the goal.

Staying Motivated

Your motivation level is probably the most important factor in determining your success. Here are strategies to get and stay motivated:

Build reminders into your life. It's surprisingly easy to lose sight of something that seemed ultra-important just hours or days before. Write down your goals and post them in a place you'll see regularly (screen savers and refrigerators were made for this type of thing!).

Focus on results. Keep your desired end result in mind. Let's say your goal is to earn an A in Organic Chemistry. There will be moments throughout the term when you may want to skip a lecture or hang out with friends rather than study. If you begin to waver, pause to think about how it will feel to get that A, and how you will be able to use the knowledge you gain from this term to move on to the next level of science.

Share. You should share your goals with at least a couple of people. Knowing that others are aware of your goals and are rooting you on will help keep you enthusiastic and accountable.

Reward yourself. Recognize and celebrate your achievements.

Teamwork

So far this chapter has focused on the individual—personal attitudes, perceptions, and goals—but much of your college experience will be about the other people you encounter. And at least some of the college experience will involve working very closely with others in teams.

Can we choose our groups? Can we pick our teams? These refrains echo down from elementary school. Chances are you've had quite a bit of experience working in groups. You've experienced the joys (or horrors) of middle school kickball team line ups. You know, the ones where a bunch of kids stand against a fence and wait for the captains to choose teams. You've seen the meltdown of a dysfunctional group, when the bickering escalates and next thing you know someone's throwing paste and glitter all over someone else. You recognize the group slacker and the group leader/dictator.

Whatever your feelings about working with teams, you will probably have many opportunities to work through them in college and in the working world, where group work is also known as just another day at the office.

In this section we'll explain what makes a good team member, describe the qualities of a successful team, and recommend strategies for getting the most out of the team experience.

What is a Team Player?

In the kickball line up the qualities that stand out are height, brawn, agility, and fearlessness. In most college classes, extracurricular clubs, and offices a team player is defined a bit differently:

Skillful. Every member of the team needs to bring some talent and skills to the group.

Cooperative. While leadership gets a lot of press, cooperation is even more important. A good team player pulls his or her weight, minimizes conflict, stays positive, and encourages others to do the same.

A good communicator. Failure to communicate well is one of the biggest sources of conflict in teams. Effective communication is essential.

Committed. A good team player lets her or his teammates know she or he is committed to the common cause and can be counted on.

Honest. Honesty is necessary to establishing trust between team members.

Responsible. Good team players share the credit, and hold themselves accountable.

Successful Teams

You have a team made up of great members. Excellent! What's the next step? To be successful, teams must possess:

Purpose. The members must understand their mission.

Empowerment. A strong team feels empowered to work and create solutions, and well-supported by their leaders and resources.

Good communication. Members should listen, speak, and discuss frankly and respectfully.

Flexibility. A good team can adapt and adjust to changing circumstances and expectations.

Productivity. A team gets the job done efficiently and effectively.

Morale. A good team keeps morale high even in high-pressure situations.

Strategies for Getting the Most Out of Working with a Team

The following are ways you can ensure success for the team:

Create clear goals. Team members must understand their goals, believe those goals are worthwhile, know what they are expected to accomplish, and understand how they will work together to achieve those goals.

Aim for small victories. Focus on small, short-term successes to build the confidence necessary to achieve the overall goal.

Build mutual trust. Trust takes a long time to build and an instant to shatter. To build trust, team members must be approachable, respectful, objective, dependable, and willing to listen.

Ensure mutual accountability and a sense of common purpose. All members must feel accountable.

Secure the resources you need. If your team is dependent on resources from outside sources, make sure they're in place before you proceed.

Develop your skills. This is the time to strengthen areas of weakness. Problem solving, communication, negotiation, conflict resolution, and writing skills are all areas where most students can improve.

Diversity

Many people think of diversity only as it relates to ethnicity. Advertisements intended to portray a business or its clientele as diverse will include images of people with a range of skin colors. But diversity encompasses much more than that and does not just pertain to visible characteristics. In fact, there are many aspects to diversity. Here are just some:

- Age
- Gender
- Ethnicity
- Cultural heritage
- Mental/physical abilities
- Mental/physical characteristics
- Sexual orientation
- Language
- Religion
- Socio-economic status

Colleges and universities around the country make it a significant part of their mission to promote, support, and celebrate diversity. They have good reason to do so. In order to thrive in the increasingly interconnected 21st century, students need to understand their own background and experience and learn about others. The world is complex and varied; a successful student will learn how to approach complexities with an open mind.

Consider these statistics:

- There are more than 450 languages spoken in the United States (Source: **www.ets.org**)
- About 10% of the U.S. population is foreign-born (Source: U.S. Census **www.census.gov**)
- 40% of American college students are "nontraditional": 25 years old or older. (Source: **studentaid.ed.gov**)

While these statistics give just a glimpse of the diversity in the United States, they provide a starting point for envisioning the college classroom of the 21st century, where students who are foreign-born and those who were born in the United States, 18-year-olds and thirty-six-year-olds, Catholics and Buddhists, students with no financial concerns and students who are struggling to pay for each term learn and work together.

The first step to becoming **culturally competent** (having knowledge of others' cultures, beliefs, perspectives, etc.) is recognizing how one's own culture and background influences one's perspective. Be aware of any stereotypes or prejudices you hold. A **stereotype** is a conventional or oversimplified image or idea.

Regional stereotypes in the United States are common: "Midwesterners are . . ." and "People from the East Coast are . . .". There are positive and negative stereotypes of different groups of people, and these stereotypes accomplish the same thing: They impose a "type" or identity on an individual. **Prejudice** is judging somebody because of a preconceived notion or opinion. ("He is an older student; therefore, he must . . .")

You'll find that if you treat people with respect and as individuals, you'll make meaningful connections and enjoy the similarities as well as differences. College is a gathering of people of different backgrounds, experiences, characteristics, and values. You have an incredible opportunity to connect with and learn from this diverse group of individuals—and to share your own experiences and perspective. **You will probably have opportunities within classes to explore points of view, experiences, and ideas that are unfamiliar to you.** Take advantage of these opportunities as often as possible. Also, **look for ways to get involved and explore diversity on your campus.**

A big part of your education will come from the things you do and learn outside of your academic requirements. You can attend classes, take notes, do the assigned work, and even get high marks, but if you aren't learning from the students and instructors around you, you'll be missing one of the most important aspects of a college education.

It's easy to surround yourself with people who are similar to you, but doing so is limiting. Challenge yourself to recognize and question your assumptions about other people, and you will be amazed at what you find. Students not only learn more about other people when they are in a diverse community; they also learn about themselves.

Keys to Success **Exercises**

1. Describe a time when you demonstrated high self-efficacy: What was the task before you? What conditions do you think led you to feel you were very capable? What was the result?

2. Describe a time when you demonstrated low self-efficacy: What was the task before you? What conditions do you think led you to feel you were very capable? What was the result?

3. In general, do you believe you have a positive perception of self-efficacy? Explain. What steps can you take to maintain or improve your perception of self-efficacy?

4. Follow the tips included in this chapter's goal-setting section to set some personal and academic goals. Explain why each goal is meaningful to you, write out an action plan for each goal, and describe how you plan to stay motivated.

5. Visit your college's multicultural center to learn more about clubs, activities, and resources available on campus and in your community. Choose one event or activity to participate in or learn about that is different and new to you. Either write a two-page reflection on your experience or share your experience with a small group of students in class.

Visit **www.LifeDuringCommunityCollege.com**
for more resources and exercises.

Health Insurance and Healthy Living

CHAPTER 8

Like anything in life, your success in school ultimately depends on your health and wellness. However, life during college—with its late nights, frequent stressors, and erratic pacing—isn't always conducive to healthy living.

In this chapter we'll cover:

- the importance of health insurance
- health insurance options
- sleep, including its benefits to mind and body
- healthful eating habits
- exercise, and why you should make it a regular part of your day
- other aspects of physical and mental health
- the flip side of health, including poor diets, stress, illness, and depression

The Importance of Health Insurance

Health insurance is a must. Even if you are young and healthy, it is an enormous risk to go without health coverage. Taking such a risk—even for a few months—could have devastating consequences.

Yes, You Need Health Insurance

1 in 6 young adults has a chronic illness, such as diabetes or asthma.

Over 23% of young adults had at least one emergency room visit in 2011.

Source: US Dept. of Health and Human Services; Centers for Disease Control and Prevention

The out-of-pocket cost of a broken ankle is over $1,500. Going to the emergency room for a sore throat, getting tested, and being told to go home and get some rest will run you about $500. (Of course, avoiding the emergency room when you do have a serious illness can cost even more.) And these examples are small potatoes next to catastrophic illnesses, which can easily rack up tens and even hundreds of thousands of dollars. Note: Under the Affordable Care Act, often called Obamacare, health insurance is mandatory for the vast majority of the population. Individuals who don't carry coverage will be fined. Exemptions to the mandate include members of some Indian tribes and individuals making less than $10,000 per year.

What coverage options are available to you?

Go to www.healthcare.gov for more information.

There are several options for health insurance coverage for a first-year college student. The first—and best—option is that you're still covered by your parents' health insurance. If this is the case, you are probably insured by either a Health Maintenance Organization (HMO) or a Preferred Provider Organization (PPO).

HMOs provide health care through a network of doctors, hospitals, and medical professionals. Participants pay a monthly premium in exchange for the HMO's comprehensive care. In order to access full benefits, participants must seek care from in-network primary care physicians and must have a referral in order to see a specialist. HMO members can usually go to out-of-network providers, but they have to pay more out of pocket to do so.

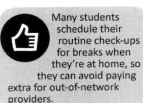

Many students schedule their routine check-ups for breaks when they're at home, so they can avoid paying extra for out-of-network providers.

PPOs have a network of preferred healthcare providers, but participants may elect to seek care from a physician outside the network if they are willing to pay more. Unlike HMOs, PPOs generally allow participants to access specialists without a referral.

The Affordable Care Act of 2010 requires insurance companies to cover their subscribers' children through the age of 26.

If your parents have health insurance, it is probably an HMO, PPO, or some variation of the two. More importantly, you can be covered on their policy up to age 26. However, if you live some distance away from home you might be out of network, which means you might not have the same coverage. This means that, while you may have relatively small co-payment requirements at your regular doctor's office back at home, any doctor in your new town will not be a preferred provider. Therefore, your share of the cost of the visit might be quite higher than back at home. To complicate matters, coverage varies from plan to plan and state to state. The best course of action is to call your health insurance company before you move to find out exactly how much coverage you'll have at college, and what you'll need to do to access that coverage. Keep a file of important customer service numbers and preferred providers in your new location.

If you are insured, do the following ASAP

- Make sure you have a copy of the insurance card
- Find out which providers in the area your insurance will cover
- Know how to access coverage, what kinds of preventive care are available, how to obtain required approvals, and how to file a claim
- Know what to do in case of an emergency

DON'T WAIT! If you get sick or hurt, the last thing you want to do is try to figure out how to navigate your insurance plan.

If you are covered by your parents' plan, they will know any time a visit is billed to their insurance.

It's much more fun to plan out your class schedule and explore the campus, but take care of health insurance business right away so you don't have to deal with it when you're sick or injured. If your parents do not have health insurance, or if the insurance they have doesn't cover you adequately in your new town, you have other options to explore:

The American Academy of Pediatrics suggests you pack the following:

- A complete health record
- A list of medicines you take
- A list of your allergies, if any
- A list of any past medical problems
- A list of any special needs you may have
- Your immunization record
- Proof of health insurance

Source: The American Academy of Pediatrics (www.aap.org)

College affiliated health insurance plans: Colleges usually contract with insurance companies to offer basic student health insurance plans. These plans have limited coverage. For instance, they often exclude routine care and they might limit catastrophic coverage to $50,000. On the other hand, student health insurance is usually quite inexpensive and can come in more than handy when you have an illness or sustain an injury. You might want to enroll in the student health insurance even if you are already covered on your parents' plan, especially if your parents' plan does not offer extensive coverage.

Federal or state insurance exchange: As of 2013, individuals may purchase affordable health care through state or federal health care exchanges. These online marketplaces offer side-by-side comparisons of various plans for comprehensive health insurance. People who make under a certain amount qualify for tax credit subsidies. Go to www.healthcare.gov to find out what's available to you.

Catastrophic coverage: The insurance exchanges offer catastrophic coverage for people who want to pay a very low premium and a high deductible. If you sign up for catastrophic coverage you'll be eligible for just a few preventative visits a year. Catastrophic coverage is better than not having health insurance, but it just protects you from, well, catastrophes.

Medicaid: If your family is low-income and you are still a dependent, you might be eligible for insurance coverage through Medicaid, which is a federal assistance program.

Health insurance is expensive, but not having it can be financially devastating. Choose a plan—or a combination of plans—that makes sense for your unique situation.

Confused yet? Here are two resources that will help you figure out your health insurance options:
www.healthcare.gov
www.statehealthfacts.org

Healthy Living

There are a lot of things to distract you from balanced meals and regular sleep habits. So it might seem comedic for us to include a section that advises, among other things, to get a full 7 – 8 hours of sleep a night, to eat healthful foods, to exercise regularly, and to limit stress. Those recommendations seem to apply to another world. College students, after all, regularly get by on only four hours of sleep. Sodium, sugar, and caffeine are considered essential nutrients, and a whole pizza counts as a little late night snack.

Nevertheless, it's worth reviewing the recommendations that mortals live by. (Or should live by, anyway.) The importance of healthy habits cannot be overstated. And, after all, this is a new phase in your life—a perfect time to establish new, healthy habits. When you have a healthy base, it's easy to recover from the occasional very late night or overindulgence.

Sleep

You've heard the recommendations on this one: 7 – 8 hours a night. But why? Why not 7 – 8 hours in little snippets throughout the 24-hour cycle? Or why not 14 hours one night a week and 4 the others?

The answer is sleep quality. People need to have consecutive hours of sleep so they can go through the necessary sleep cycles. While you sleep your body and brain are busy releasing hormones, restoring energy, and doing other work that will make you smarter, stronger, and more alert the next day. Good sleep improves learning, performance, mood, and health. There are countless studies to support the importance of sleep—and that detail the negative effects for those who don't get enough or whose sleep isn't of high quality.

To maintain good sleep habits:

Go to bed and wake up at the same time every day. Erratic sleep patterns can lead to insomnia and other problems.

Nap. Research shows that short naps can actually make you more alert and enhance your performance.

Plan. When you plan well, you can avoid all-nighters. Studying all night won't help you absorb information anyway, so you might as well study efficiently during your alert hours and enjoy your sleep.

Avoid showers, baths, and exercise the hour before bedtime. They are stimulating and make it difficult to get to sleep. Caffeine, alcohol, and some medications also inhibit sleep.

Exercise. Do exercise, but don't do vigorous exercise in the three hours before bedtime as it will keep you awake.

Make your room sleep-friendly. Get the temperature right, minimize light and noise, and make your bed comfortable (and not just an extension of your desk).

Eating

Very few people intend to gain weight while in college. It just happens, sneaking up ninja-like. You likely have work, responsibilities at home, and now reading and homework to do too. Throwing your schedule out of whack can easily get the healthiest person off track.

The best way to avoid sudden weight gain is to be aware of your diet and to know the basic facts of good nutrition. You may want to consider using a fitness and diet app like Myfitnesspal or Myplate to help you track your progress.

You've heard it before, but let's review and make some simple, manageable goals that even the most harried college student can follow:

Six Easy Nutrition Goals

GOAL #1: Choose a good "default" breakfast. This should be a standard, healthy breakfast that you can eat almost every day. That way you won't have to make decisions about breakfast and you won't end up skipping it—two things that can kill your goal. If you have an early class, breakfast should probably be something you can prepare quickly. Good options: Instant oatmeal, toast with peanut butter, a hearty cereal with milk and a banana, or eggs and fruit.

GOAL #2: Make meals a part of your daily routine so that you don't get ravenously hungry and end up digging into a personal pan pizza.

GOAL #3: Pack healthy snacks (almonds, raisins, fruit, etc.) to classes and study sessions.

GOAL #4: Keep a water bottle with you and drink from it regularly. Benefits: You'll stay hydrated; you won't get thirsty and mistake the thirst for hunger; you won't be tempted to drink empty calories; you'll have a place for a cool sticker that the cute student next to you will ask you about and then he or she will ask you what you're doing after class.

GOAL #5: Eat 5-9 servings of fresh fruits and vegetables a day. The benefits: You'll get vital nutrients AND you'll be filling up on good things, making the other stuff just a little less tempting.

GOAL #6: Read nutrition labels. The cafeteria's chicken pot pie might sound great until you read its stats. Make informed decisions.

There's a lot more to know about nutrition, of course, but these goals can help you start some basic good eating habits. Also, check out these online resources: **www.choosemyplate.gov** and **www.nutrition.gov**.

Exercise

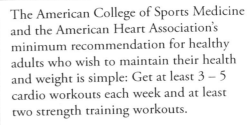

The American College of Sports Medicine and the American Heart Association's minimum recommendation for healthy adults who wish to maintain their health and weight is simple: Get at least 3 – 5 cardio workouts each week and at least two strength training workouts.

It seems like the easiest thing to do, yet we all know how quickly exercise can slip to the bottom of the priority list. You don't need a gym to get a good workout. You don't even need to do the full workout at once.

What you do need is motivation, so here are some reasons to follow the recommendations:

Exercise:

- increases energy
- helps you get a better night's sleep
- reduces stress
- increases self-confidence
- reduces your risk of heart disease, high blood pressure, and diabetes
- makes you look and feel great
- is fun!

Here are some ways to make exercise a regular part of your life in college:

Schedule time to exercise. If it's a priority—and it should be—it needs to be on your calendar and as fixed as an appointment you would make with another person.

Develop a realistic exercise plan that you can follow. It's better to work out half an hour a day six days a week for a semester than to work out three hours each day for a week, then give it up.

Join a community sports team or gym. Have fun, meet people, and stay in shape.

Find an exercise partner. Having a friend who commits to exercise with you is a great way to stay motivated and on track. (Sometimes, literally on the track!)

Choose to move. Walk or bike to class instead of taking the bus or driving. Walk up stairs instead of taking the elevator. Choose dancing or bowling rather than watching a movie. Play a sport instead of watching a sport on TV.

Consider using a wearable activity tracker to keep you motivated, track food, exercise, steps, and sleep.

Stress

Stress can be a positive. It can motivate and encourage creativity, for instance. On the other hand, if not managed well, stress can cause mental, physical, and emotional strain. Left unchecked, high stress can lead to health problems such as anxiety, depression, weight gain, headaches, and high blood pressure. Stress is inevitable, but here are some strategies you can adopt to minimize its impact.

1) Recognize the signs of stress, which may include:

- Dramatic weight loss or gain
- Headaches
- Fatigue
- Diarrhea
- Problems sleeping
- Muscle tightness or spasms
- Frustration, nervousness, irritability, and mood swings
- Lack of interest in things you used to enjoy
- Loss of concentration
- Forgetfulness
- A feeling of being overwhelmed

2) Know the common stressors of college life:

- Exams and assignments
- Grades
- Studying
- Relationships
- Time demands and scheduling conflicts
- Uncertainty about the future
- Finances

3) Get a handle on stress:

Practice good organization and time management. Planning well will help you avoid situations that lead to stress, such as forgotten appointments, overdue assignments, and lost items.

Shift your perspective. What will this stressful event feel like a week from now? Next year? In 5 years?

Break overwhelming projects into smaller, more manageable tasks. Instead of cleaning your entire room in one day, for example, set the goal to clean out the closet one day, and the rest of the living space the following day.

Stay healthy. Sleep, eat right, and exercise.

Take a break. When you're feeling overwhelmed, take time to think about it and do other things.

Be good to yourself. Don't beat yourself up over things. Make sure you reflect on the things you do right and focus on how you can use that self-knowledge in the future.

Play. Take time to have fun. It will release stress and give you perspective on the things that are causing your anxiety.

Meditate. Research shows that mediation boosts immune function and decreases anxiety and depression. Even a few minutes of meditation a day can help you manage stress.

Get help if you need it. Just because stress is common doesn't mean it's too trivial to discuss with a counselor. If it's negatively affecting you, seek professional advice.

Illness

The stressful, often erratic college lifestyle can make college students especially prone to illness.

Reduce your risk of illness by taking the following measures:

Have an annual physical.

Make sure your vaccinations are up to date.

Cover your coughs and sneezes, and wash your hands often.

Handle food with care. If you're not sure how long that yogurt's been sitting out, err on the safe side and toss it. For food safety guidelines, including storage times for refrigerated food, go to www.foodsafety.gov.

Don't overuse antibiotics. Use antibiotics only when necessary and only when prescribed to you. If you are prescribed antibiotics, finish the entire course of the drug to ensure that the illness has been fully treated.

See a doctor or physician's assistant when necessary. Ignoring symptoms won't make them go away and it won't make the underlying condition any easier or cheaper to treat.

Depression

You already know that depression can be triggered by a negative event like the loss of a loved one, serious physical illness or injury, a failed relationship, or a series of bad grades. But what about a positive event, like starting college? Starting college is an exciting time and will likely require you to make changes to your life. For some people life transitions can cause anxiety and even depression; after all, facing new challenges and a new routine can seem overwhelming.

Often, depression is inherited and individuals with a family history of depression may be more likely to suffer from depression themselves. Sometimes depression isn't attributable to any particular cause, but is brought on by a combination of circumstances.

The good news is that depression is a treatable illness. If you are experiencing any of the following symptoms, you should seek help from your physician or counselor:

- Persistent sad, anxious, or "empty" mood
- Feelings of hopelessness or pessimism
- Feelings of guilt, worthlessness, helplessness
- Loss of interest or pleasure in activities you once enjoyed
- Decreased energy, fatigue, feeling slowed down
- Difficulty concentrating, remembering, or making decisions
- Insomnia, early-morning awakening, or oversleeping
- Appetite changes and/or weight loss or weight gain
- Thoughts of death or suicide
- Restlessness, irritability
- Persistent physical symptoms that do not respond to treatment, such as headaches, digestive disorders, and chronic pain

National Crisis Hotlines

Important numbers to know if you or a friend needs information or help:

National AIDS Hotline
1-800-CDC-INFO (1-800-232-4636) (Center for Disease Control)

Alcohol and Drug Abuse
1-800-729-6686 (Substance Abuse and Mental Health Services Administration)

Cutting and Self-Abuse
1-800-DONT-CUT (1-800-366-8288) (Self Abuse Finally Ends organization)

Eating Disorders
1-800-931-2237 (National Eating Disorder Organization)

Pregnancy
1-800-230-PLAN (1-800-230-7526) (Planned Parenthood Hotline)

Rape, Sexual Abuse, and Incest
1-800-656-HOPE (1-800-656-4673) (RAINN Rape Crisis Hotline)

Suicide Hotline
1-800-273-TALK (1-800-273-8255)

Health Insurance & Healthy Living
Exercises

1. Make sure you have a current copy of your health insurance card. If you moved for college, check with your insurance company to find out which area providers are in your network. If you do not have health insurance, go to www.healthcare.gov to find out about insurance options for you.

2. Keep track of your sleep for a week. How much sleep do you average per night? Is it high quality sleep? Do you feel well-rested after a night's sleep?

3. Tour your local gym. What are its hours of operation? What kinds of classes are available?

4. Describe your support system. What do you do when you get sad or stressed out? Make a list of steps you can take reduce your stress and prevent becoming overwhelmed. If needed, seek out professional counseling through your insurance company or local agencies.

5. If a loved one exhibited signs of depression, what steps would you take to get him or her help? Discuss with a group.

Visit **www.LifeDuringCommunityCollege.com**
for more resources and exercises.

Housing Options

Unless you already have a place to call home during this transition into college life, you'll need to figure out your housing situation. Some community colleges offer on-campus housing, but most do not. This chapter will walk you through housing options and related issues, including:

- choosing housing: on- vs. off-campus housing
- finding the right apartment
- understanding your lease
- tips for moving in and out

On-Campus Housing

If you attend a school with on-campus housing available, that housing is maintained, operated, and subsidized by your college. While most on-campus housing is located on the campus, some colleges—especially those in urban areas—maintain housing facilities on properties that are not actually part of the campus. Common types of on-campus housing include:

Residence Halls
Residence halls are usually multi-story buildings featuring rooms that are shared by two, possibly three, roommates. Each residence hall floor usually has a kitchen and living area as well as a suite of bathrooms that is shared by all the residents of a floor.

Suites
Some dorms are divided into suites—apartment-like sections of a building. A suite may consist of two to four bedrooms connected by a common living area with a kitchen and shared bathroom.

Student Apartments or Townhouses
These are living situations modeled after off-campus housing. They are just like an apartment or townhouse and are usually very popular. (Hmm, perhaps because you don't have to share a bathroom with forty other people?)

Family Housing

Some colleges offer housing specifically designed for students who are married and/or who have children. Family housing is often similar to student apartments or townhouses, and may include amenities like a day care center and playground.

When you do have a choice of whether or not to live on campus, consider these pros and cons:

Pros	Cons
CENTRAL LOCATION: On-campus housing is close to everything you need—your classes, the dining hall, campus recreation, etc.	**NO CHOICE OF ROOMMATES:** Many colleges assign roommates, though some will allow student input in the process.
NO COMMUTE: You can walk, bike, or take a campus shuttle to get around easily.	**FEWER OPTIONS:** Depending on your college, you may have a limited list of living arrangements in comparison to off-campus options.
SERVICES: On-campus living usually includes conveniences such as custodial services, trash pick-up, pest extermination, and repairs.	
SUPPORT: You will have a handy support network of resident assistants and advisors, the campus housing office, and other resources.	**LIMITED PRIVACY:** Shared facilities and group living is part of the on-campus living experience—and one you may not love.
COST-EFFECTIVE: Once you add up all the services included in your housing fees and subtract the hidden costs of living off campus (for example, commuting costs, grocery bills, cleaning supplies, etc.), living on campus can be more cost-effective, especially if your college is in an upscale or urban area.	**MEAL LIMITATIONS:** If your housing includes a meal plan, you might tire of the restrictions of on-campus eating, such as hours of operation and choices of food.
ALL-INCLUSIVE: You will not have to worry about bills for heating, air-conditioning, electricity, water, gas, or sewer. Many colleges also offer free Internet and cable.	**RULES AND REGULATIONS:** To maintain order, protect property, and ensure students' safety, colleges set and enforce all kinds of rules and regulations.
SAFETY: Crime occurs everywhere, but on-campus housing generally has more security resources available.	**LIMITATIONS ON GUESTS AND PETS:** Most campus housing bans pets, and many have rules about how many visitors are permitted.
RESERVES & NATIONAL GUARD: For students affiliated with the Reserves or National Guard, on-campus housing contracts are easy to break should you be called up to active duty and forced to withdraw from school. Many colleges have a formal policy to handle activations, so be sure to check with your Veterans Office for more information.	**PARKING RESTRICTIONS:** Parking on campus near your residence hall may be restricted and/or inconvenient.

Off-Campus Housing

Your options for off-campus housing are varied and range from leasing an apartment with a roommate in an apartment complex, to renting a home with a group of friends, to renting a room in a family's home.

Off-campus living has both an up and a down side:

Pros	Cons
MAY BE LESS EXPENSIVE: On-campus housing includes a lot of services, which may make it more expensive than your off-campus options.	**MAY BE INCONVENIENTLY LOCATED:** You'll be—by definition—off campus, and may have to trek quite a way to get to your classes.
CHOICE: You get to choose where to live, your roommate(s), and what kind of living situation fits you best.	**MORE MAINTENANCE:** Some landlords require that their tenants mow the lawn. Others will expect you to deal with some problems—such as cockroaches—that arise. The expectations will depend on the situation, but you'll certainly have more maintenance with an off-campus situation.
SPACE AND AMENITIES: You might get a more spacious apartment, and one with more bells and whistles.	
PRIVACY: Because you can choose your living situation, you can elect to have a private bedroom and even a private bathroom. Also, it may be easier to find quiet time to study, sleep, and relax.	**MORE RESPONSIBILITY:** No custodians. No oversight. You will need to remember to take out the trash, clean the fridge, and pay the electric bill.
INDEPENDENCE: Fewer rules = more freedom.	**HIDDEN EXPENSES:** Toilet paper, cleaning supplies, groceries, commuting costs, your own furniture—the costs add up fast.
PETS AND VISITORS ARE WELCOME (possibly): Many landlords maintain restrictions on pets, but some will allow your furry or feathered friends. And speaking of friends...in off-campus housing you won't have someone standing over your shoulder counting how many visitors come by.	**COMMUTING:** If your off-campus home is not close to campus, you will have the added hassle of commuting.
	LESS SUPPORT: Off-campus housing does not come with a resident advisor or campus housing office. Some landlords may be difficult to work with, and you'll be on your own for any negotiations or issues.

If you do decide to live off campus, you'll need to figure out exactly what kind of apartment you want. Sit down with your roommate(s) and make a list of the features and services that are essential to all of you, as well as a list of those things you'd like but don't really need, and the things you'd like to avoid. Then set a price range you can afford.

Here are some things to think about:

Location: How close do you want to be to campus? To grocery stores? To the bus or subway line?

Safety: What areas of town are considered safe? Are the units of the apartment well maintained and up to code?

Size: How many bedrooms and bathrooms do you need? How big of a kitchen will suit your lifestyle?

Features: Do you want a place with a yard? A balcony? Air conditioning? Charm?

Amenities: What kinds of things can you not live without? A laundry room? Cable television? A security system? A pool or workout facility?

Rules: Every landlord and apartment complex has its own rules. Do the rules of the apartment you're considering match your lifestyle?

Furnished or unfurnished: You may have the option of renting a furnished apartment, which can offset the cost of living off campus. Do you need furniture? Are you happy with the furniture that's provided?

What do others have to say? Get good intel by checking with other students about recommended places to live. Also, do research online. Many websites, such as Yelp and Google Reviews, provide thorough information about apartments and leasing companies, along with tenants' reviews.

After you and your roommates agree on the kind of apartment you want, it's time to start looking. Check out the classified section of the newspaper, Craigslist and other Internet sites, local apartment search services or property management companies, and bulletin boards on campus and around town. Also, drive or bike around town to get a feel for the different neighborhoods and to find potential rentals that haven't been listed yet.

Negotiating with a Landlord and Signing a Lease

Remember the law of supply and demand? It is about to have a direct effect on your life. If there are lots of apartments available in your college community, you will be able to leverage a better deal. If not, you will have to compete with other renters and will need to compromise. One thing you can do to give yourself more leverage is to maintain an excellent credit score, as your credit rating affects your ability to lease as well as the amount of deposit required and the rent price.

Here are a few things you can do to negotiate a better rental deal, even in a scarce market:

Sign an extended lease. If you know you love the property and can commit to staying in it for longer than the minimum lease, let the landlord or property management company know. Landlords love the stability of having good tenants stay for over a year and yours may give you a reduction in rent or security deposit in exchange for signing an extended lease.

Know the rental market. Research the going rental rate for apartments in your area and what kinds of amenities and features you can get for what kinds of prices. Don't be afraid to talk with a landlord about what other complexes or buildings are charging or offering, and to negotiate a better rental rate.

Haggle the deposit. The deposit is one area where landlords may be willing to make allowances because it will, most likely, be returned to you at the end of your rental agreement. Ask if your deposit can be reduced or paid in increments over several months.

Don't just think money. Reducing your rent is ideal, but you may also consider asking the landlord for other allowances, like replacing the fridge or repainting.

Consider asking for a month-to-month lease. Ask the landlord if you can extend your lease on a month-to-month basis once the terms of the original lease are up. This can give you flexibility in the future and help you save on the costs of putting a security deposit down on a new apartment and moving again.

After you have come to an agreement with the landlord on the terms of your rental, go over the written lease very carefully to make sure it reflects your agreement. Before you sign your lease:

Read it carefully. You should ask if you can take the lease home to review it in private. This will give you time to read it word for word—and to enlist the help of a more experienced friend or family member if you need it.

Highlight any concerns and ask for clarification. If there is anything in the lease you do not understand, that concerns you, or that you feel contradicts your oral agreement, highlight that section and insist that your landlord clarify it. In some cases, he or she will have to revise the document before you sign.

Make sure your written lease is identical to your oral agreement. If your landlord promised you new carpet, make sure it's written down. If she said she would waive the pet fee, make sure it's written down.

Moving In and Moving Out

Some college students end up in legal wrangles with landlords or former landlords, which is inconvenient and expensive. Protect yourself by taking the following precautions:

When Moving In:
Conduct a thorough walk-through before moving in. Inspect every aspect and feature in the apartment and make a detailed list of its imperfections: stains, holes, outlets that don't function, broken windows or mirrors, crooked cabinets, nonworking appliances, etc. Ask your landlord to sign your completed list, and then make a copy for each of you.

Make sure it meets your standards. If the apartment has not been cleaned, repaired, or doesn't meet the specifications outlined in your lease, inform the landlord and request that the necessary adjustments be made immediately.

When Moving Out:
Conduct a thorough walk-through with your landlord or the property manager before you move out so he/she can indicate any potential problems, such as damage or alterations.

Have your landlord sign off on a statement outlining what you will be charged for, if anything, and stating when and how your deposit will be returned to you. This is a critical step—students have been surprised by bills for damage many months after they vacated an apartment.

Have a question about your rights as a tenant?

 Go to your state's attorney general's website to search for tenant rights.

Leave it like you found it. It's good manners and it makes sense to leave the property in as good of shape as you received it. First, you want to establish a good list of references for future rentals. Second, you want to recoup all the money you put down as a deposit.

Special Circumstances

The possibilities are endless, so we'll cover a few of the most common special circumstances you might encounter:

Free-rent promotions. In a saturated market, apartment complexes and landlords will compete for your money. You will see all sorts of promotional programs, including free rent for a certain number of months. Read the fine print and ask the important questions. If you're satisfied that it's a genuine deal, go for it!

Special discounts. Some landlords and property managers offer special discounts to veterans and their family members, employees of specific companies, or members of particular groups. Check to see if that's the case in your new apartment, and ask if the special discount applies to you.

Bartering. If a landlord just has a few properties, he or she might be willing to exchange services for reductions in rent. You might landscape, paint, or do other work and save some much-needed cash.

Subleasing. Because college students are not always able to fulfill the full term of their rental agreements, there may be a variety of subleasing opportunities available to you. Subleasing can sometimes be a good deal because the original renter may be in a tight spot and willing to rent the property for less than he or she is paying. Also, you might not have to pay a deposit in a subleasing situation.

Servicemembers Civil Relief Act (SCRA). For members of the National Guard and Reserves, the Servicemembers Civil Relief Act provides a wide range of protections, including a provision to terminate your lease, when called to active duty. If you find yourself needing to break your lease due to activation, check with Legal Services and the Veterans Office at your college for assistance.

Housing Options Activities **Exercises**

1. With a partner or in a small group, review the two pros and cons lists at the beginning of this chapter. What pros and cons would you add to the on-campus list? What pros and cons would you add to the off-campus list?

2. Create a list of the things you would need, want, and not want in a rental property.

Must have	Want to have	Must Not have

3. Do a little field work to figure out: 1) Where you can find out about housing availabilities in your community, 2) Areas of the community where you would like to live, 3) The price range of off-campus living options, and 4) Where you can find information about the landlord/tenant laws in your state or city.

Visit **www.LifeDuringCommunityCollege.com**
for more resources and exercises.

Roommates

If you're like most first-year college students, your roommates up to this point have been family members. There were probably power struggles, breaches of privacy ("Oh! Dad! I didn't know you were still in there!"), and miscommunications. There was also probably love and affection. And squabbling siblings. Moving out on your own can be so difficult and such a relief—and then you realize you aren't really on your own at all. You have a roommate (or two or three) and life is about to get very interesting.

You might end up being best friends with your first-year roommate, but don't even consider it yet. The first thing to do is simply to establish a friendly relationship that includes freedoms and responsibilities for both people. This chapter will include:

- a description of a good roommate
- recommendations for developing a good relationship with your roommate
- strategies for dealing with difficult roommate situations

The Good Roommate

Chances are you didn't have to worry about being a good roommate back home. If you weren't one, Mom or Dad or a sibling was right there to remind you of your duties and check your attitude. You knew the rules of the house and everybody's boundaries. Living with a roommate is different because 1) you haven't grown up with him/her, 2) you won't have the usual cues to remind you of your household rights and responsibilities. Good roommates...

Show consideration. Good roommates are considerate and think about their impact on the people around them. They respect their roommate's rights, property, and independence. They appreciate their roommate's individuality—including culture, religion, political beliefs, values, musical taste, and appearance. Good roommates show gratitude and appreciation.

Compromise. Good roommates are willing to do what it takes to make the living situation pleasant for both people. They keep reasonable hours or, if they don't, they don't let their late nights or early mornings affect their roommate. They respect their roommate's right not to have a constant stream of visitors.

Are accountable. Good roommates are accountable for their behavior, admitting when they are wrong, owning up to mistakes, and working to resolve problems.

Communicate well. Good roommates speak to each other respectfully and are willing to listen.

Be a good roommate and expect your roommate to be the same. If he or she isn't, we have some tips for dealing with difficult situations later in this chapter.

Tips for Living with Roommates

Just like any new relationship, it's important to get off to a good start with your new roommate. Here are some tips for doing just that:

Get to know your roommate. Try to contact him or her before the move-in date if possible. We recommend calling your roommate. Students have shared with us how awkward some first connections have been because they relied on social media correspondence or texting. Speaking of social media, if you do become "friends" with your roommate in this medium before you actually meet her or him, remember the limitations of the format and, well, don't judge. Once you feel comfortable with your roommate, you can begin discussing your living arrangements, including the kinds of items each of you will bring (no need for two microwaves—there will hardly be space for one!). If you and your roommate live near each other, try to meet up before the big move-in day.

> **Roommate Resources** 🔍
>
> For sample and printable roommate agreements, check out these sites:
>
> **www.tidyforms.com**
>
> **www.shakelaw.com**

Keep an open mind. Forget about your dream roommate (and forget about your nightmare roommate, too). Whoever you meet will broaden your perspective of the world and your understanding of people. Try not to make assumptions.

Don't expect too much. You may end up being close friends with your roommates, but it's not a given. On the other hand, sometimes roommates are very compatible because they don't spend all their time together.

Establish rules. Some colleges publish a roommates' bill of rights and responsibilities that clearly outline the "rules of engagement" of rooming together. Even if your college doesn't produce such a publication, make sure you and your roommate sit down early on and establish rules to live by. Your rules should cover the use of the television, radio, or other technology in shared spaces; sharing clothes and other personal items; quiet time for studying and sleeping;

cleanliness and cleaning duties; guests, including overnight guests; privacy.

Communicate. Communication is essential to a functioning roommate relationship. Let your roommate know if something is bothering you about the living situation; also, let him or her know if you are appreciative of something he or she did.

Respect your roommate. Every successful relationship is rooted in respect—respect for each other's individuality, privacy, property, opinions, and values. Living with someone different from you is not always going to be easy, but you will learn from it.

Important Roommate Conversation Starters:

What are our pet peeves?

What are our sleep schedules?

When and how do we study best?

How should we talk to each other if we have a problem?

Do we want a lot of visitors? A few? How do we feel about overnight guests?

What stuff will we share? What stuff is off limits?

How much noise can we tolerate? How much quiet do we need?

What are some definite "no nos" in our room? (e.g., smoking, drugs, accordion playing)

Source: Adapted from Syracuse University's orientation material

Dealing with Difficult Situations

You've heard the horror stories. And, while those stories make great anecdotes years later, you might be able to avoid them altogether. Here are some scenarios to help you deal with difficult situations:

Living with a friend or relative. It sounds ideal to live with someone you already know and trust, but it doesn't always work out well. In fact, living with a friend can be even more difficult than living with a stranger because friends have higher expectations for each other than strangers do. Make sure you establish expectations and rules and maintain respect for each other.

Changing roommates. Sometimes a living situation is unbearable and an issue is not resolvable. If you live on campus, know that some colleges will allow you to change roommates, though you may have to wait until the end of the term or until another living arrangement becomes available. Review your college's policies regarding roommate changes, and contact your resident advisor or housing department to find out more. Before taking this action, however, make sure you've done everything in your power to try to resolve the situation yourself.

Living with roommates off campus. Off-campus living is attractive—the freedom, the cool houses, the non-cafeteria food. If you and your roommate decide to live off campus you won't have the support network of the housing department and resident advisors. You will be on your own to pay the bills, fulfill the lease requirements, and care for the apartment. These responsibilities can add to tension between roommates, so do your best to map out a plan for dealing with off-campus living issues.

Living with more than one roommate. Multiple roommates mean a cheaper monthly rent and a lot of potential miscommunications. There are additional rules to keep in mind when it comes to living with more than one roommate:

- **Don't gossip or backstab.** It's easy to fall into the trap of talking about one roommate behind his or her back. If you have issues or problems, go straight to the person who can actually help resolve them—the source.

- **Don't gang up.** If you need to approach a roommate about a particular issue, do everything possible to ensure he or she doesn't feel like you and the other roommates are ganging up on her or him.

- **Be honest.** Fess up if you ate the last piece of pizza. Acknowledge when you haven't done your share of the dishes.

Legal issues. Very rarely, college students find themselves in situations that are bigger than they can deal with alone. Sometimes roommates steal property, refuse to pay the rent, commit illegal acts on the premises, or even threaten their roommates. If you suspect that your living situation has become dangerous or that your roommate is involved in unlawful activity, seek help immediately to keep yourself safe and on the safe side of the law. If you live on campus, your resident advisor should be able to help or point you to a resource that will help. If you live off campus, you may need to seek the help of your landlord, law enforcement or college legal assistance.

Roommates **Exercises**

1. With a partner or small group, draft a Roommate's Bill of Rights and Responsibilities. When you are finished, compare your draft to other students' drafts. If your college has a Roommate's Bill of Rights and Responsibilities or a similar document, compare your draft to that, too.

2. If you haven't done so already, talk to your roommate about which expectations you share, where the two of you might need to compromise, and how you can prevent awkward situations.

3. Write a letter to future college students about how to get to know your roommate—and what not to do!

Visit **www.LifeDuringCommunityCollege.com**
for more resources and exercises.

Homesickness

The high school student afflicted with so-called "senioritis" likely interprets the term "homesick" as "sick of home." By spring of senior year, many students think of home as a place to change clothes, grab some food, and engage in the occasional argument with their parents. But things change. And in the fall those same people who couldn't wait to leave often become the first-year college students who ache to be home again, and who write despairing posts about it.

The symptoms of homesickness vary and may appear before you even hang up the first poster in your new place. You may feel uneasy, dissatisfied, annoyed, unsure of yourself, sad and lonely. And the fact that you're feeling these things now, when you've finally made the much-anticipated transition may make you even more uneasy, dissatisfied, annoyed, etc. Sure, you knew you'd miss the good things—the dog, free cable, and other perks. But who knew you could also miss your dad's corny jokes or that strange sinister voice your mom uses when she wakes you up to do chores on a Saturday morning? How can something be so annoying in May and so poignant the following September?

Starting college is a lot like moving to another country. Whether you're a one-hour drive or a cross-country flight away from home, you have to figure out new customs and a new language. It's dizzying: a whole new set of friends, a new town to explore, and the ability to sleep in as late as you want (provided you schedule your classes right). The freedoms of college life are overwhelming. And then there are the real stressors: Challenging classes, roommate issues, and figuring out how to finance the whole experience. So much is unfamiliar that, naturally, you long for that most familiar place: home.

The only sure cure for homesickness is to move back home. However, there are other less-extreme remedies that will allay the symptoms. This chapter will:

- explain why students get homesick

- give you ideas for coping with homesickness

Understanding Homesickness

Homesickness is actually a form of separation anxiety that can occur at any time during a person's life. You may have experienced it on the first day of kindergarten or your first sleepover. The circumstances that cause this anxiety vary from person to person and age to age, but it's important to know that people well into adulthood may experience anxiety, obsessive thoughts, and even mild depression during times of transition. And your first year in college *is* a major transition point.

We all hear how college is supposed to be the "time of your life" and, when you look around, it might seem like other first-year students are enjoying every minute of their college experience. Don't worry about what you "should" be feeling or what you think other people are feeling; that will only add to your stress. Instead, recognize how you *do* feel and realize that it's normal.

> **Homesickness** does not always feel like sadness or nervousness. Sometimes, homesick persons feel angry, irritable, or disoriented.
>
> From: "Preventing and Treating Homesickness," Christopher A. Thurber, PhD, Edward Walton, MD and the Council on School Health. Published in Pediatrics (Volume 119, Jan 2007).

Coping with Homesickness

There's no cure for the ailment of homesickness, but here are seven ideas for ways to cope with it:

1. Get busy. Free time is great—if you're not lonely. If you are, you might spend that free time counting and recounting the days remaining until Thanksgiving break, and then the days remaining until Winter break, and then…. Instead, challenge yourself to pack your daily schedule with activities. Try an intramural sport, join a few clubs, attend the concerts and games around campus. Doing so will help you feel more connected to your new community. Then, when you do go home for a break, you can really relax (and maybe even miss school a bit).

2. Talk. Reach out to friends, your resident advisor, your chaplain…anyone who will listen to you and help you feel more connected to your new home.

3. Stay in touch, but be where you are. Skype, text, call, and email your family and friends back home. Just don't let staying in touch keep you from making new friends and experiencing college life in real time and real space.

4. Bring a little home with you. Display reminders from home—photographs, special objects, music—in your room. Also, try incorporating a routine from home into your new life. If, for example, you watched a certain TV show every week at home, watch it in your new home, too.

5. Be good to yourself. Lack of sleep, a poor diet, and no exercise are sure ways to amplify feelings of sadness and stress.

How Astronauts Deal with Homesickness

Who could feel more separated from home than an astronaut? Here are some tips found on NASA's website:

- Stay connected. Family video conferences and frequent news updates are just two of the ways NASA psychologists help the astronauts feel connected to home.

- Stay busy. Two hours of exercise a day, space walks, data collection, experiments, the occasional malfunctioning equipment, not to mention the extra-long time it takes to brush one's teeth in space...it's no wonder one astronaut says the time "flies" by.

Source: **www.nasa.gov**

6. Let yourself be sad. Homesickness is natural, so don't get down on yourself for it.

7. Think about moving back home. Some students get to campus and feel exhilarated, then stranded. Remember that you're not stuck: you can switch at semester's end or at the end of the year. It is a choice that you made and you have the choice to stay or go. Simply reflecting on that fact can give you perspective on your homesickness. Many students consider the alternative of moving home and realize that they still prefer the new, exciting, and slightly spooky experience of being away from it.

Feeling homesick is a natural part of the transition to college. It won't necessarily go away, but you can learn to deal with it. And when you're back home for holidays, chances are you'll appreciate it more at first, then begin to miss the college life you've made for yourself.

Homesickness **Exercises**

1. Have you felt or are you feeling homesick? Rate the severity of your homesickness on a scale of 1 to 10, where 1 represents no longing for home and 10 represents a severe longing for home. What times of day and what circumstances seem to evoke feelings of homesickness for you?

2. Brainstorm a list of 5 action steps you could take this week to make yourself feel more at home at college.

Visit **www.LifeDuringCommunityCollege.com**
for more resources and exercises.

Social Media and You

CHAPTER 12

What is power? Consider the whistleblowers who can, with a few anonymous posts, leak information that shakes up a huge corporation or a government. Or the community that, after being devastated by a natural disaster, rallies and organizes assistance through tweets and Facebook posts. Or the college student who can, with a green screen and a cheap camera, transform himself into a popular movie critic. Thank social media for all of that.

As with all forms of great power, there's a flip side. Social media makes it possible to connect with loved ones, acquaintances, and strangers who share your interests; it also makes it possible for other people to paint a one-sided picture of you that's hard to control. It allows information to spread quickly, but that information might be incorrect or damaging. Social media is also quite deceptive: the "little guy" can turn him or herself into a powerful voice for his or her cause; the bully can be a jerk 24/7 to a huge audience. And, of course, social media can be addictive and a waste of time. But you already know this, right?

In this chapter, we'll discuss:

- connecting with friends and family via social media
- building a good online presence—now and into your future
- risks of social media
- ways to improve privacy and security online

Connecting via Social Media

As a 21st century college student, you have broad reach. You can connect easily with all sorts of people and groups and maintain those connections. It can give you a platform for building relationships with other students, instructors, and even alumni. Social media also makes it simple to stay in touch with everyone at home.

Incidentally, one challenge you'll have as a first-year student might be connecting to your new environment with the people right next to you. You know, the *physical* ones.

Imagine! You can be at a huge party surrounded by new friends and you can video chat with your parents at the same time! (OK, you might not want to be connected with everybody all the time.)

In fact, one of the big benefits—and possible drawbacks—of social media for the first-year college student is staying tethered to home. It can help ease the pain of homesickness because you can see your loved ones—at least on a screen—as often as you want. Touching base with what's familiar, whether it's the sound of your Dad's voice or a picture sent from your best friend, may help you feel happier and more ready to engage with the unfamiliar. It can also make homesickness worse, though, if you are so tied to the people *back there* that you don't take time to connect in real time to the people and places *here*. Or, you might find yourself wanting to immerse yourself in your new surroundings, but someone back home texts you twenty times a day and wants to Skype every evening. For some students, such frequent communication with home is a joy and for others it's a pet peeve. Don't be surprised if the first few months of college are an adjustment period as you figure out how to live at school and "visit" home, rather than "living" at home and visiting school.

Your (Online) Identity

If you are like 94% of your peers, you already have an online identity. You've probably been using Instagram and Twitter for years and have already built an online presence. But here's a concept many people who use social media are just beginning to grasp: FOREVER. Your online presence will stick around for a lot longer than the technology you're using to drive it. There's no shame in acting childish or saying things we wish we hadn't, but the Internet isn't a forgiving place. Things stick around. No need to panic, but there are some things you need to know to keep your personal identity and your online identity under control.

In this section we'll discuss how to manage your online presence so that it helps you in the future rather than holding you back.

First, take stock of your current online profile. Here's a handy exercise: Google yourself to see what others can easily find out about you. Odds are, you've already done this exercise on someone else. See anything interesting? If you end up with a few innocuous results (your little league batting average or a graduation picture, for instance), you are in a great position, as you can simply monitor your online presence and make sure nothing gets linked to your name that you don't want. You'll also want to build on that presence, which we'll get to in a moment.

Second, delete or bury content, if necessary. If you do have blog posts, pictures, or other items online that could potentially embarrass you or limit your chances of finding and keeping a job in the future, simply delete them, if possible. It's not likely that you can remove the images or content from every source, but you can try to bury it by increasing favorable content. For instance, some people use LinkedIn, Twitter, or Pinterest, because activity on those websites makes their most relevant and recent content most visible. It's no different from what many companies do to help their brand.

Another way to bury negative items is to create a new website or blog and add to it regularly.

Finally, think about your future online identity. What do you want future connections, colleagues, employers and potential employers to learn about you when they search for you online? They do check. You can build up a professional presence with LinkedIn and Twitter and following those organizations that relate to your academic interests. For example, a student passionate about marine biology might become a digital advocate for the group Ocean Conservancy. Connecting with organizations you're genuinely interested in will keep you up to date on the latest news in your field and might also lead you to internship opportunities. Who knows, your social media savvy might compel the organizations you're interested in to hire you to manage their own social media presence. It happens all the time.

Make an Impression with Online Posts or Tweets

Job recruiters are impressed by:

- Affiliations with professional organizations
- Volunteerism

Job recruiters are turned off by:

- References to drugs, alcohol, and sex
- Profanity
- Poor grammar and spelling mistakes

Source: Jobvite, 2014

Don't worry if you don't have your professional goals all figured out at this stage. If you do know what you want to do when you graduate from college, you can start building a more specific professional presence online now. If you aren't sure what you want to do next semester much less in four years, you can still establish a foundational professional presence online now.

Social Media Risks and Ways to Improve Privacy and Security

What are the risks of social media? Our engagement on social media starts with taking a risk: we give up certain privacy in order to connect with others or have access to something we want. Once you're in, it's simply a matter of limiting or increasing your risk.

Behaviors that increase your risk:

- Posting personal information, including phone number, address, and date of birth

- Posting personal plans (for example, when you're leaving town, which route you're traveling)

- Sharing images and text that you'd be embarrassed about if they got out or existed forever (assume both will happen)

- Password and PIN laziness: As we discussed in Chapter 4, you want strong passwords even if they're hard to remember

- Not using privacy settings and not paying attention when privacy settings change

- Clicking before thinking. If people paused before clicking, there would be fewer victims of scams (Best Buy is giving away free televisions!!! Click "like" and submit your name and email address to claim yours!!) and fewer apologies necessary (Sorry about previous tweet. My info was wrong.)

Unfortunately, there are some things out of our control entirely. People have had their lives turned upside down by all sorts of jerks, some of them criminal and some not. For example, in addition to the scammers, phishers, and catfishers, there are people who create social media accounts in others' names and use the platform to bully. There are others who repost sexy or obscene pictures (real or edited) and try to charge the victim money to remove them.

> **Carnegie Mellon researchers found that public information easily found online can be used to predict an individual's social security number.**
>
> Source: Carnegie Mellon, 2009

It's revolutionary, evolving, pervasive, and powerful. While social media modes change quickly, they all satisfy a basic human need: to communicate. Unlike the days when humans gathered around the fire pit, however, the communication now is easily replicated and archived forever. We have just hundreds of cave paintings from early humans, and millions of silly pet videos from modern humans. Whether you use social media to entertain or to inform, whether you use it to create or curate, use it wisely.

Social Media **Exercises**

1. Google yourself and note the top twenty hits your search yields. What would someone else learn about you if they were to Google your name?

2. Consider your social media use. How much of it is dedicated to consuming content? To creating content? To curating content?

3. Working with a small group of classmates, discuss the use of social media in your classes: How are professors integrating social media tools? How are students it to work together? How are students using it to learn or conduct research?

4. Working with a small group of classmates, discuss what you see as an up-and-coming social media site or platform. What makes it appealing? What are its potential uses?

Visit **www.LifeDuringCommunityCollege.com**
for more resources and exercises.

Military Veterans and Service Members

CHAPTER 13

Developed from excerpts of *Life During College: The Veteran's Guide to Success* (2015), written by Dr. Nicholas J. Osborne.

If you're a veteran you're no stranger to transition and the ability to adapt and overcome. Throughout your military career, you not only received training and developed expertise, you may have also endured deployments, separation from loved ones, and a move every couple of years. As a veteran, you value taking risks and having a mission, which makes you an ideal candidate for this new task of succeeding in higher education. This chapter will discuss the following topics that relate specifically to veterans in college:

- Military culture and college culture
- What it means to attend college as a veteran
- Student veteran strengths, as well as pitfalls to look out for
- Resources on campus
- Education benefits
- State and federal resources
- Career resources

Military Culture and College Culture

Generally speaking, core aspects of military culture include

- Discipline
- Organized hierarchy and rank system
- Communication that is direct and to the point
- Irregular work hours and a possibility of hazardous conditions
- An emphasis on teamwork, not individualism
- Not talking about your problems ("Suck it up and drive on…")

Veterans arrive at college after having spent a good portion of time living and working within a unique culture. Military culture, after all, is highly structured, with its own customs and policies—not to mention its own alphabet and a dictionary of acronyms! Civilian society and life on campus may seem like a different world at first.

Training and education in the military focuses on practical application rather than theory, and it often takes place as a regimented group activity. In college, however, education is more self-directed: you attend class on your own and are responsible for creating your own study schedule. In the military, you simply can't be late for a training. In college, missing class or arriving tardy might not even be noticed. Developing sound time management and independent study skills, then, is paramount for being a successful college student.

Attending College as a Veteran

Whether you have decided to get additional training for a specific career or whether you seek personal enrichment and knowledge, there is a reason you have decided to go to college. As a veteran you are a nontraditional learner, which means you are different from many of the other students on campus, who may have just recently finished high school. Although you may not be much older than your classmates, the disparities in your life experiences will likely set you apart. Also, because you had a break from education due to your military service, it is very common to feel uncertain or anxious about being a student, particularly when thinking about math or writing papers.

Veterans differ from traditional students in the following ways:

- Veterans are often older
- Veterans are more likely to have at least one dependent, such as a spouse or child
- Veterans are more likely to be less involved in campus-based activities
- Veterans often work while attending school
- Veterans are more likely to have a documented disability
- Veterans often report feeling "rusty" when going back to school

Student Veteran Strengths

Veterans are unlikely to be homesick and are comfortable working in diverse environments. Unlike your civilian peers, you have likely spent time living in various locations. Also, you have worked and served with people from a broad range of ethnic, cultural, and socioeconomic backgrounds.

Veterans are disciplined and reliable. From getting up early for physical training to working long and irregular hours, veterans know what it means to be on time and to stay on task until the job is completed.

Veterans are hard working. Many veterans joke that a 40-hour work week is an easy week. Veterans know the importance of paying attention to detail and of doing things in the exact manner in which they've been trained.

> Now that I'm a student I'm concerned about a lot of things, like remembering how to study for a test since I've been out of school for a long time. I'm also worried that I won't relate to my classmates because I'm older and have already had a career.
>
> **Chris, Marine Corps Veteran**

Veterans know how to adapt. Structured deployment training cycles, being in the field or on watch, and sleeping in cramped or dangerous places—veterans know how to adapt to conditions and their environment.

Veterans are resourceful. Veterans know how to make do with less. From being sleep deprived and hungry to having the wrong tools for the mission, veterans know how to be resourceful and meet their objectives.

Veterans are mature. The military demands its members take their jobs seriously. Although many veterans attend school in their 20s and 30s, their unique life experiences have matured them.

Pitfalls to Look Out For

Too much too soon. The culture of the military expects you to learn quickly so you can assist your team. This often means putting in long hours to study, train, and prepare for a mission. One of the biggest pitfalls veterans encounter, particularly in their first year in college, is the "too much too soon" syndrome. For example, a veteran might enroll in too many credit hours or in a course sequence that is disproportionately challenging (e.g., all math and science courses). Or he or she might try to cram a bunch of material into a short period of time, such as studying all night before an exam instead of preparing for it in stages.

Isolating. You may find that it is hard to relate to your younger classmates or it may be challenging to get involved in campus activities. Although many veterans treat college like a job, it is important to blend your academics with other interests and not to isolate yourself. A student veteran organization can be a great way to meet similar peers and engage in a variety of social and service-based activities.

> It's very important to reach out to your college's VA Certification Official or VA Center early on. Know your contact person and have him or her help you determine if you're maximizing your benefits.

Not knowing what resources are available. Your college is a vast environment with different types of offices and resources. Take the time to learn about the different support services available. (We'll discuss some of those in the next section.)

Not asking for help. Military culture often shuns asking for help. Many veterans feel pressure to not "burden" people when they need help but it is inevitable that at some point in your college career you will need guidance. Don't think of this as being a burden—think of it as getting the resources you need to accomplish your mission.

Neglecting self-care. You know how to study for hours without a break, skip meals, and keep charging, but at some point you will hit a wall. To prevent burnout be sure to incorporate fun and fitness into your routine.

Resources on Campus

We discussed a range of general college resources in Chapter Two. Here, we'll discuss how some of those resources relate specifically to veterans, as well as other resources that are only for veterans.

Veterans Office

To accommodate the growing number of veterans in higher education, many colleges have a designated veterans office to serve as a bridge and support student veterans with their transition to college. The veterans office can offer advocacy in areas related to VA education benefits, federal work study opportunities, housing, academic services, and peer mentoring. It can also provide referrals to other campus-based and community offices. Be sure to contact the veterans office as soon as you enroll in school!

Disability Support Services

For wounded and injured veterans, an acquired disability is a new experience. Disability Support Services offers academic and other important support to students with a range of disabilities and learning differences. It determines eligibility, informs students of their rights, facilitates academic accommo-dations, works with other campus offices to ensure accessibility, and provides education about disability management and self-care.

> It is important to contact Disability Support Services before starting class. Waiting until the exam or assignment is due is too late and will cause more stress. Have your official accommodations on file before class starts.

It is important for a student veteran to know that campus-based disability services are not tied to the military or Department of Veterans Affairs in any way. For example, a veteran may have a disability rating with the VA, but this information will only be available to a campus disability office if the student veteran authorizes it. Conversely, using disability services on campus will not in any way impact their VA rating or result in additional financial compensa-tion. They are two separate "worlds" and will not share information without the written consent of the veteran.

So, what are the advantages of using a campus disability office? Many veterans find that they experience anxiety before a test or that they need to take exams in environments that minimize distraction. Additionally, some veterans attend college with a brain injury and/or post-traumatic stress. A campus disability office can provide testing and offer various types of accommodations for a range of conditions along with individualized services.

Financial Aid

The Veterans Certifying Official at your college will likely be housed in this office and will serve as the central contact for setting up your VA education benefits.

Counseling Center

Because of an increase in service members attending college, many campus counselors have received specialized training and are familiar with veterans' diverse needs.

Tutoring Resources

Most schools have a tutoring center, as well as writing and math support, free of charge. The VA will also provide financial assistance for veterans who need individual tutoring services. For more information, go to **www.benefits.va.gov/gibill/tutorial_assistance.asp**

Honors Program for Veterans

High achieving veterans are eligible to join SALUTE in addition to their college's Honors program. SALUTE is a national honor society for veterans. For more information, go to **salute.colostate.edu**

Student Legal Services

Most colleges offer some form of free or reduced-cost legal services. Common issues students bring to this office include tenant-landlord disputes and consumer complaints. If you are affiliated with the National Guard or Reserves while attending college, this office may be helpful if you are mobilized to active duty and need to break your lease.

Education Benefits

Many benefits are available to advance the education and skills of veterans that will ultimately support their career goals. Spouses and family members may also be eligible for education and training assistance. Some veterans find that they're eligible for more than one benefit or that one program is more suited to certain education and training goals than another. To learn about the various education and training programs administered by the Department of Veterans Affairs, we recommend that you begin your search by visiting the "Get Started" webpage: **www.benefits.va.gov/gibill/get_started.asp**. And be sure to visit your campus Veteran's Service Center. The team in this office is very familiar with available benefit programs and the steps to necessary to acquire them.

DOD Military Tuition Assistance

http://www.militaryonesource.mil/education-and-employment/higher-education-for-service-members

Military Tuition Assistance is a program under the DOD which offers funding of up to 100% of college tuition for active service members. Each service branch, the Coast Guard, National Guard and Reserve Component are eligible and maintain their own application process.

- Army (www.goarmyed.com)
- Marine Corp (www.marines.com/being-a-marine/benefits/education)
- Navy (www.navycollege.navy.mil/)
- Air Force (www.my.af.mil/)
- Coast Guard (www.uscg.mil/hr/cgi/active_duty/pay_for_college/ta/default.asp)

Post-9/11 GI Bill
www.benefits.va.gov/gibill/docs/pamphlets/ch33_pamphlet.pdf

The Post-9/11 GI Bill offers higher education and training benefits to veterans, service members, and their families who served after September 10, 2001. If you have at least 90 days of aggregate active duty service after September 10, 2001, and are still on active duty, or if you are an honorably discharged veteran or were discharged with a service-related disability after 30 days, you may be eligible for this VA-administered program.

Montgomery GI Bill
www.benefits.va.gov/gibill/montgomery_bill.asp

The Montgomery GI Bill assists active duty and Reservists with the pursuit of higher education degrees, certificates, and other education and training.

Reserve Educational Assistance Program
www.benefits.va.gov/gibill/reap.asp

REAP provides educational assistance to members of the Reserve components called or ordered to active duty in response to a war or national emergency declared by the president or Congress. Note: according to **www.military.com**, "The REAP program has been terminated for all new applicants, it is scheduled to terminate completely in November of 2019."

Veterans Educational Assistance Program
www.benefits.va.gov/gibill/veap.asp

VEAP is available if you elected to make contributions from your military pay to participate in this education benefit program. The government matches your contributions on a 2-to-1 basis.

Survivors and Dependents Educational Assistance Program
www.benefits.va.gov/gibill/survivor_dependent_assistance.asp

The Dependents' Educational Assistance (DEA) program offers education and training opportunities to eligible dependents of veterans who are permanently and totally disabled due to a service-related condition or of veterans who died while on active duty or as a result of a service-related condition.

Student Veterans of America
www.studentveterans.org

Many colleges have a Student Veterans of America chapter that works closely with the veterans office to provide resources and support to student veterans. The SVA is the student veteran voice on campus and their entire mission resolves around advocacy for service members. An SVA chapter is a great way to meet other veterans and learn more about your college from a peer's perspective. Many SVA chapters also spearhead a variety of social and philanthropic activities that support veterans in their communities

Veterans Upward Bound
www2.ed.gov/programs/triovub/index.html

This free U.S. Department of Education programs designed to motivate veterans and provide refresher training in key subject areas. Many colleges participate in VUB and provide mentoring along with individual instruction with the goal that veterans will complete their postsecondary education program and enter into meaningful fields.

State and Federal Resources

State Veterans Office
www.va.gov/statedva.htm

Each state maintains a designated office for veterans. Many states also provide county representatives who provide information on benefits. A variety of scholarships and grants for veterans and their dependents may also be available through this office.

Department of Veterans Affairs
www.va.gov

The VA has a multifaceted mission to support veterans in several ways. Navigating the VA can be tricky and overwhelming given the vast number of services provided. Based on this, the veterans office at your college or in your county is an excellent starting point for getting individualized guidance and coming up with a plan. While getting started, refer to the links below for an overview of services and eligibility.

Summary of VA Benefits
benefits.va.gov/BENEFITS/benefits-summary/SummaryofVABenefitsFlyer.pdf

VA Education Benefits
www.benefits.va.gov/gibill/

VA Healthcare Benefits
www.va.gov/HEALTHBENEFITS/index.asp

Vocational Rehabilitation & Employment
www.benefits.va.gov/vocrehab/

VA Regional Office Finder
benefits.va.gov/benefits/offices.asp

Vet Center Program
www.vetcenter.va.gov

The Vet Center Program provides a range of readjustment counseling services to eligible veterans and their families in an effort to support a successful transition from the military to civilian life. Because many college-based counseling offices only offer a limited number of sessions to their students, a Vet Center is an excellent resource for ongoing services. Another advantage of a Vet Center, aside from being free, is that you will be working with clinicians who are experienced working with military populations. Services provided through Vet Centers include:

- individual and group counseling for veterans
- family counseling for military-related issues
- military sexual trauma counseling and referral
- substance abuse assessment and referral
- employment assessment and referral
- screening and referral for medical issues including traumatic brain injury, depression, and post-traumatic stress

Give an Hour
www.giveanhour.org

Give an Hour is a nonprofit organization that provides free mental health services to veterans and their families affected by the conflicts in Iraq and Afghanistan. These civilian providers include counselors, social workers, psychologists, psychiatrists, and others.

1-877-WAR-VETS Call Center
1-877-WAR-VETS is a 24-hour confidential call center where combat veterans and their families can talk about their military experiences or any other issues they are facing in their readjustment to civilian life. The staff is comprised of combat veterans from several eras.

National Resource Directory
https://m.nrd.gov/

The NRD is a comprehensive directory that provides access to thousands of services and resources at the national, state, and local levels to support recovery, rehabilitation, and reintegration. Service members, veterans, family members and caregivers can find information on key topics such as health care, employment, education, and counseling. Their handy search engine allows you to locate resources by state and zip code.

Military One Source
www.militaryonesource.mil/

Military One Source is a confidential Department of Defense-funded program that provides thorough information on many aspects of military life at no cost to active duty National Guard and Reserve members, and their families. This is your source for information about deployment, financial and legal issues, education and employment benefits, and a host of other categories.

Community Veterans Organizations
Community-based veterans organizations are excellent resources for meeting other service members, learning about the area, networking, and getting peer to peer support. The links below will assist you finding a local chapter in your community.

American Legion
www.legion.org/

Veterans of Foreign Wars
www.vfw.org/

Marine Corps Association and Foundation
www.mca-marines.org/

Military Officers Association of America
www.moaa.org/

Iraq and Afghanistan Veterans of America
iava.org/

Career Resources

Veterans' Preference
According to the U.S. Department of Labor Veterans' Employment and Training Service (VETS), veterans who are disabled or who served on active duty during certain specified time periods or in military campaigns are entitled to preference over others in hiring for virtually all federal government jobs. And as a bonus, many state and county jobs also award veterans' preference!

Check out this brochure for more information:

www.dol.gov/vets/Education%20and%20Outreach/Program%20
Brochures/PREFERENCE.pdf

CareerOneStop
www.careeronestop.org/

Sponsored by the U.S. Department of Labor and a partner of the American Job Center network, CareerOneStop provides support with identifying employment that matches your skills and interests, information on salary ranges for specific careers, and a robust job search engine.

Department of Labor Veterans' Employment and Training Service (VETS)
www.dol.gov/vets/

VETS is a robust resource that administers programs to meet the employment and training needs of veterans and eligible spouses. Here you can explore career options, translate your military experiences into civilian language, and receive specialized guidance on searching for a rewarding career.

Disabled Veterans of America (Veterans Job Search)
www.dav.org/veterans/veterans-job-search/

The DAV offers free assistance from specially trained National Service Officers to link service-injured or ill veterans to job training and job assistance programs.

G.I. Jobs: Jobs for Veterans
www.gijobs.com/

This site provides an updated list of "hot jobs for veterans" in addition to highlighting strategies for identifying careers of interest and coordinating a job search.

Hire Veterans
http://www.hireveterans.com/

The name says it all. This active job board connects veterans to industry leaders. Job seekers can also post their resumés and access a collection of career-based resources.

Military.com
www.military.com/

This expansive site is a go-to for finding resources for job search, skills translation, resumé building, career advice, job fairs, transition support and employers looking to hire veterans.

Military-Friendly
www.militaryfriendly.com/

A division of Victory Media, this helpful site provides an exhaustive list of schools and employers designated as "military-friendly"

MilitaryHire: Jobs for Veterans and Transitioning Military
www.militaryhire.com/

This site has been developed and is maintained by a team of military veterans and corporate hiring authorities.

Veterans bring a wealth of experience and knowledge to higher education and the workforce. They have developed the discipline and mindset that allows them to adapt to their immediate environment. They are also accustomed to putting in the hours and dedication necessary to get the job done. However, even super-heroes have their vulnerabilities and areas for growth. For veterans, feeling a bit out of place or rusty is a normal part of the transitional process as is trying to muscle through without assistance. Developing a positive routine early on and identifying helpful resources are paramount for success.

Academic Planning

CHAPTER 14

Crafting your academic plan requires a good bit of self-reflection as well as forecasting what you see yourself doing in the future. It is a process of exploration that involves asking questions, setting goals and taking action while constantly assessing your progress along the way.

To get started, consider the following questions: What kind of job would I enjoy going to each day? What types of subjects hold my interest? Is my area of interest best suited as a hobby or a career? How can I match my education to my long-term goals?

This chapter will discuss the following:

- Your academic advisor and you

- Selecting a major and minor

- Changing your major

- Developing a graduation plan

- Selecting and registering for classes

Your Academic Advisor

Your academic advisor is an invaluable resource to keep you on course when you're navigating the college landscape. Ideally, your academic advisor is an approachable, caring, knowledgeable mentor who will inform you about options and requirements and help guide you in your decision making. Usually, your advisor is assigned to you. He or she might be a full-time professional advisor or a professor in your chosen field of study who also advises students. At this early stage your "chosen field" is whatever box you checked when you sent in your initial paperwork.

Selecting a Major

Check with your student handbook or your academic advisor for your college's requirements regarding selecting a major.

Selecting a major may be a carefully weighed decision, it may be a leap of faith, or it may be a little of both. You will find a variety of advice when it comes to deciding on your path to graduation and beyond. Some say "follow your bliss." Others say "follow the money." Only you can decide what is best for you.

Take tests. Visit your Counseling Center or Career Center and see what types of aptitude and personality tests are offered. Identify your strengths and interests.

Make a list. Write a list of the topics, classes and careers that interest you.

Do research and ask questions. What types of majors and minors stand out for the careers you're interested in? What percentage of graduates actually end up working in a field related to their major? What is an average starting salary for a specific major?

Talk to the experts. Talk to people who work in a field you find interesting. Check out your college's Career Center or Alumni Office – the staff can put you in contact with all sorts of resources, including alumni who have volunteered to mentor students.

Get hands on. Nothing beats hands-on experience for finding out what you like. Check with the Career Center and speak with faculty about work-study and volunteer opportunities and internships.

Consider the Career

Where can you go and what can you do with your major? While you may love the content of business management classes, if the thought of leading, advising, and managing people terrifies you then Business Management is not the major for you. When selecting a major, carefully consider what kinds of career options it would lead to. Also, be sure to think about technology and how it can impact a career. Some majors and occupations are quickly becoming obsolete, while others are up and coming and are forecasted to grow.

> *The greatest obstacle to discovery is not ignorance—it is the illusion of knowledge.*
>
> Daniel J. Boorstin,
> American Historian

Evaluate your personality. How does your personality suit your major's career options? Are you a people person or do you prefer working with numbers and facts? Are you a team player or someone who works better alone? Do you thrive on change or crave routine?

Map out the educational commitment. Many careers require more education after the initial college diploma. You may have two, four, six, even seven more years of classes, residencies, apprenticeships, and so on.

Consider career conditions. What kinds of hours do you want to work? Would you thrive in a profession that has busy and slow seasons? Do you like to work on tight deadlines and in a fast-paced environment? Do you like autonomy or would you feel comfortable working within an organizational structure?

Evaluate earning power. Some professions have higher earning potential than others. How important is money to you and your future? What kind of lifestyle would you like to have and what kinds of commitments and sacrifices are you willing to make for it? The U.S. Department of Labor has all sorts of interesting information about careers on its website, including how much various professions make, and what the projected need is for workers in those professions: www.onetonline.org

Hot Jobs! Here are some of the fastest growing professions, according to the Bureau of Labor Statistics:

- interpreters/translators
- genetic counselors
- physician assistants
- statisticians
- audiologists
- physical therapists
- nurse practitioners
- operations research analysts

Source: www.bls.gov/ooh/fastest-growing.htm

Changing Your Major

Many students begin working on one major and then switch after they discover something new and exciting about another major or after they realize that their current one isn't the right fit. You can change your major. In fact, the average college student will change his or her major at least twice. The more frequently you change majors and the later on in your education you make the change, the more costly it gets. You might graduate later than you planned or pay for classes that were unnecessary to your degree. However, switching majors in college is less costly than completing one degree and then coming back to school years later to earn the degree you really want.

Selecting a Minor or a Double Major

Selecting two majors or a minor is a good way to get the most out of your college experience. Of course it can be difficult and time-consuming, too. Before committing to a double major or a minor, consider the following:

Decide as early as possible so you can develop a good course schedule and graduate in a timely manner.

Limit your electives. Because of the number of classes required to fulfill a double major or a major/minor, your schedule will not have room for many electives.

Select thoughtfully. Do your majors complement each other? Will the combination add to your range and career choices? How much time will it take you to complete the degree?

Think of your academic plan as a work in progress: in the first year it's very malleable. With flexibility and foresight—and some help from your academic advisor and others—you can customize an academic plan that has room for experimentation *and* graduation.

> *I'd rather fail at doing something I love than succeed at doing something I hate.*
>
> **George Burns,**
> **American humorist**

Developing a Graduation Plan

Some students decide on their major, then schedule exactly those courses they need to graduate. They know their destination and they take the Interstate to get there: It's direct and fast. Others take a bit longer to decide on a major or they choose to pursue additional degrees. This is like traveling with a general idea of your destination and taking a combination of major highways and scenic byways to get there. A few students truly meander or are diverted by time, interest, or money and graduate later than their peers. The time it takes you to graduate is up to you and your interests and circumstances. No one gets a medal for coming in first. On the other hand, it can get pretty expensive to take classes that don't relate to your major or minor. It's handy to have a map, even if you don't end up following it precisely the way you intended to. Here's how to develop a graduation plan:

Use the course catalog. Most college course catalogs provide sample graduation schedules. You can create your individualized plan based on these examples.

Pay attention to prerequisites. Upper level classes usually have prerequisites, classes you are required to take before you move on. Make sure you fulfill the prerequisites early on so you'll be able to fit in all the courses required for your major.

Check in with your advisor. Your academic advisor knows the big picture and the little details, as well as insider information like which classes are really exciting but have a dull title.

Sample some classes. If you are unsure about the major you want to pursue, take introductory courses that will give you a sampling of the majors you are considering. This way you'll broaden your experience and find the major that really sparks your passion. Another way to explore your options is to audit a course or sit in on a couple of class sessions.

Don't miss out. Some classes are offered on a rotating basis: fall semester only or spring semester only. Others are offered sporadically. Sometimes there's an incredible professor who teaches a course once every other term or so. Find out about these special offerings—check with your advisor or ask other students—and plan accordingly.

Achieve balance. Easier said than done, we know! Balance in this context means registering for a combination of difficult and easier courses each term to avoid unnecessary stress. It also means regulating your credit load: Refer to your college's recommendations for the number of credits per term. You don't want to overload and burn out or perform poorly in that term; you also don't want to take so few credits that you lose momentum or lose out on financial aid.

Consider summer school, online classes, etc. You now have the option to take classes anytime and anywhere. Taking a couple of classes during the summer will give you more flexibility during the school year.

Selecting Classes

Ah, the course catalog! So many possibilities! How should you choose which classes to take?

Find out what's required. Most colleges have undergraduate minimum requirements that all students must fulfill. You will also have required courses in your department once you've declared a major. Check and double check the course catalog to make sure you're taking the right classes at the right level. Your academic advisor will help you evaluate your high school transcript and college entrance exams to determine what course levels you should begin with.

Research the course. Start by reading the full description in the catalog. If you need more details, contact the department or instructor or go to the relevant website. Talk to your advisor and to other students who have taken the course. You may find reviews online or in a campus publication—these can be helpful, but they can be misleading, too. Course reviews are by nature subjective. What another student calls "impossible and confusing" you might call "challenging and intriguing." Is the instructor good? Is the class easy? For some students these are the same questions, for others they're quite distinct.

Research the instructor. Word gets around: This instructor is incredible! That professor's lectures are amazing! You'll hear about instructors who inspire and provoke, who challenge students and change lives. Their teaching style might be traditional or avant garde, their classes might be lecture-based or experiential, but there's something about them that makes an impression on students. Try to sign up for such classes when you have a chance even if they don't fulfill a requirement—the worst thing that could happen is you take an awesome class from a great teacher, the best thing that could happen is you discover a passion for a subject you didn't know about before. If you hear through the grapevine about an instructor who is ineffective, follow up on that information with more research. There are some classes that you might want to avoid. You only have so much time and money and you want to make the most of your education.

Graduation Planning Calculator

Adventures in Education, a service of the Texas Guaranteed Student Loan Corporation, has a great online calculator that students can use to budget their time in college—as well as their finances. **www.aie.org**

Challenge a course when appropriate. If for some reason you are not satisfied with the course level you were assigned, you may want to challenge a course. This usually involves taking a placement exam that covers the material that would normally have been presented in the course. If you pass the exam, you are not required to take the course and can move on to higher level classes. Most colleges levy a fee for the process of challenging a course—and a student will have to pay the fee whether or not their challenge is successful. Also, if you do pass the exam you may have to pay for being awarded credits for the course.

Again, check with your advisor before beginning the process.

Registering for Classes

The process of registering for classes varies from campus to campus. Classes can get filled or canceled. Based on this, build your ideal schedule in advance, knowing that you'll need to be flexible on the day of registration. Here are other things to keep in mind as you create your schedule:

Some colleges offer priority registration for veterans.

Your commitments. Do you have a work schedule? Family commitments? Extracurricular activities? Make sure you plan your classes accordingly. If you will be working until midnight most nights you probably don't want to schedule an 8:00 a.m. class. If you have a major life event coming up, you may want to limit the number of challenging classes you take that term.

Your biological clock. The one that tells you to wake up at 5:00 a.m. and feel drowsy at 3:00 p.m. (or vice versa). By now you know when you're most alert, most able to learn, and most energized. Schedule classes and homework time for those hours, if possible. It's easy to find energy to play Ultimate Frisbee or to chat with a friend, but it's difficult to muster energy to sit through hundreds of slides of ancient artifacts—if those hundreds of slides are projected onto a screen in a dark, warm room when you're at your sleepiest.

What's Your Prime Time?

When am I most alert?

When am I sleepiest?

What's my most productive time of the day?

When am I least focused?

Visit **www.LifeDuringCommunityCollege.com**
for more resources and exercises.

Your downtime. You need to get from one class to the next. You need to eat. You need to study. (OK, maybe studying doesn't count as downtime. But "non-class time" has a certain awkwardness to it, so we'll file it in this category.) Be deliberate about your class schedule *and* your break schedule.

Do everything in your power to create an ideal schedule, make sure your bills and fines are paid up (sometimes the most miniscule fine can keep you from registering!), preview the registration process, get instructor approval for those classes that require it, have your pins and passwords handy, and register the very moment it's open to you.

The Filled Class

Have alternative course times available when registering for your classes in case your first choices are not available.

You researched and planned. You tapped in the right numbers at the right time and...you were denied. The filled class is one of the frustrations of the first year of college. One remedy is to take a breath and see what else is available. If you really have your heart set on that class, you can contact the instructor directly and ask if he or she would be willing and able to make an exception. Or you can ask the instructor if she or he will allow you to attend the class through the add/drop period and take the spot of a registered student who decides to drop the course. You may even be able to register for an open section of the course, but attend the lectures of the closed class. Make sure your instructor is on board with this switch and confirm that the lectures and content for the two classes are identical before you attempt this creative approach.

Academic Planning **Exercises**

1. Review all the majors your school offers and research at least two that interest you. What are the credit requirements for each major? What kinds of prerequisites are there for each major? Which classes in the subject seem particularly interesting? Which classes in the subject seem particularly difficult or not interesting? What kinds of internships or apprenticeships are related to each major? What kinds of career opportunities are there?

2. Which resources were most helpful in answering the questions above?

3. Take an aptitude or personality test at your college career center or counseling office. Or, if those tests are unavailable on campus, take one online at **www.mynextmove.org/**. Reflect on your results: According to the test, what are your strengths, weaknesses, personality traits, and interests? Which education or career paths do the results suggest for you? What did you learn about yourself (or about the test) through this process?

4. Outline your ideal week: When would you attend classes? When would you study? What extracurricular activities would you do and when? When would you sleep and eat? How much time would you spend socializing and what kinds of socializing would you prefer? What other things would you do with your time?

5. What resources are available to find out more about a class or instructor at your college?

Visit **www.LifeDuringCommunityCollege.com**
for more resources and exercises.

Learning Styles

Hollywood's vision of learning includes agonizingly dull lectures (think *Ferris Bueller's Day Off*: the economics teacher intones, "The Hawley-Smoot Tariff Act, which… anyone?....Raised or lowered? ….Did it work?...anyone?") as well as inspiring classrooms where passionate teachers shout, "Stand up! Stand on your desks!" The teacher either numbs or transforms. The students are either stunned by boredom or awestruck. What's missing from many of these fictional versions of school is the students' active role in their own self-transformations.

> *When the student is ready, the master will appear.*
>
> **Buddhist Proverb**

You will have inspiring, passionate instructors, but don't wait for someone to leap onto a desk and recite poetry. You are your most important teacher. A successful student knows that and knows how to learn. He or she is open to new ideas, engages with and reflects on her experiences, and seeks challenges. In this chapter we'll:

- provide a brief overview of the learning process
- give examples of individual learning styles and complementary study strategies
- discuss the importance of being an active learner and a critical thinker

The Learning Process

What is learning? Definitions of learning abound and sometimes contradict each other. There are theories, charts, seemingly paradoxical explanations ("learning is the act of unlearning"), models and wikis.

We'll keep it simple here and focus on one widely used and referenced definition, and suggest resources if you'd like information about others. Learning is, according to David Kolb, a professor at Case Western Reserve University and an influential educational theorist, "the process whereby knowledge is created through the transformation of experience. Knowledge results from the combination of grasping and transforming experience." Kolb's model of experiential learning involves action and reflection, experience and abstraction. Students may process information differently and prefer one mode over another, but the best learning occurs when students—and instructors—integrate all four modes. Here is an adaptation of the learning construct Kolb describes:

ACTION	REFLECTION
Learn by doing. **Put theories to the test, relate concepts in your own way.** Examples: Papers, projects, creating models	**Learn by thinking about what you've heard, seen, experienced, etc.** Examples: Discussions, journaling, brainstorming
EXPERIENCE	ABSTRACTION
Learn through direct involvement. Examples: Field work, labs, simulations, homework	**Learn by observing and reading.** Examples: Attending lectures, reading the textbook, thinking about concepts

Successful students involve themselves in concrete experiences, reflect on their experiences (reflection), create concepts and theories based on their reflections (abstraction), then test those theories (action). Learning, then, is a process and each step builds on the previous one. People don't necessarily learn in a specific order—some move from abstraction to action, for example—and many students exhibit a preference for one of these modes of learning.

Which category or categories seem like a good match for you? When you bring home a bookshelf from IKEA, are you more likely to take all the pieces out and get right to work (action) or read the directions thoroughly (abstraction) before you even consider picking up that little Allen wrench? After wrestling the new bookshelf into place, will you reflect on the experience? (Hmm, maybe next time I should wait for my roommate to help me!)

Discovering Your Learning Style

If you're interested in identifying and exploring your learning or personality type, there are plenty of resources to assist you. They range from long, detailed inventories to quick questionnaires. These tools can help you articulate your strengths and weaknesses, give you insights into how you relate to other people, and suggest majors and professions that might spark your interest and play to your strengths. However, you should also know that there is much debate in the education community about the validity of categorizing learning styles. That said, we'll share one popular model with you for your information—and leave it up to you to decide how helpful it might be.

One popular model of learning styles proposes that people prefer learning through Visual, Auditory, or Tactile/Kinesthetic modes. For example, a visual learner might be more likely to retain information from class when it is presented with film and images. A visual learner might need to sketch out a concept in order to understand it, and would benefit from using color-coded notes and flash cards. A tactile/kinesthetic learner, on the other hand, might learn more from hands-on activities and labs, and could use rhythm to help memorize information.

You probably already know quite a bit about how you learn and have discovered from experience that what works for you doesn't always work for other people. Take a look at the following table. Which characteristics do you recognize in yourself? Are you more of a visual learner, an auditory learner, a tactile/kinesthetic learner, or are you a combination of learning types? What can you add to the "Learns Best From" column? Which of the recommended learning strategies have you already tried? Which ones work best for you? Which ones will you try?

	Characteristics	Learns Best From	Learning Strategies
Visual Learner	• Learns by seeing • Thinks in pictures • Prefers written directions • Draws ideas on paper • Remembers faces • Imagines scenes and characters in books • Seeks out pictures and graphs to understand material • May not retain auditory information for long	• Lectures with images • Diagrams, charts • Pictures • Films	• Write out notes and lists • Create pictures and diagrams to understand and retain information • Use graphic organizers • Color-code notes and study guides • Make and use flashcards
Auditory Learner	• Learns by hearing/talking • Attentive to discussions • Prefers verbal directions • Remembers names • Sensitive to intonation, pitch, and tone of voice • May be distracted by noise	• Lectures • Discussions • Presentations and speeches	• Read explanations, directions, and study notes out loud • Form study groups and discuss class material • Use audio books • Create rhymes and songs to help remember material • Record lectures and review them
Tactile/ Kines- thetic Learner	• Learns by doing/feeling • Expresses self through movement and gesture • Remembers activities • Prefers to experiment, figure things out • May have difficulties reading and spelling	• Hands-on activities • Experiments and lab work • Skits, role-plays, and performances	• Use rhythm to memorize information (e.g., pace while reviewing flash cards) • Create models of concepts and information • Make and use flashcards • Visualize using physical sensation cues

Learning Style & Personality Type Surveys

Discover yourself (and put off writing that research paper)!

Kolb Learning Style Inventory

Learning and Study Strategies Inventory (LASSI)

VARK Learning Style Inventory

Multiple Intelligence Inventory

Myers-Briggs Type Indicator (MBTI)

These are just some of the popular learning style and personality type surveys. A few are available online; others may be available through your college's career or counseling office.

Active Learning and Critical Thinking

More important than your preferred learning style and your dominant personality traits is whether you are an active learner. Here we mean cognitively active rather than jumping-jacks-in-the-lecture-hall active. Do you ask questions, either out loud in class or internally as you read? Do you anticipate outcomes? Do you propose theories? Do you follow your curiosity? Do you reflect on your understanding of a topic and identify gaps in your knowledge? Do you look for biases in your own thinking and in others'? Do you synthesize new information with previous knowledge? The active learner does all of these things all of the time. In fact, the term "active learner" is redundant: A learner does all these things all the time.

The passive learner, by contrast, simply consumes information. To the passive learner, a lecture is like a TV show, and a lab is just a series of actions one must imitate. The term "passive learner," then, is a misnomer, as there is no real learning taking place in these examples.

One of the hallmarks of an active learner is the ability to **think critically**. According to Edward Glaser, co-author of the *Watson-Glaser Critical Thinking Appraisal* (1941), Critical thinking requires a certain attitude, a body of knowledge, and skills:

Attitude: The critical thinker considers ideas and information in a thoughtful way. The word consider comes from the Latin considerare, meaning "to inspect closely, to observe." A critical thinker's attitude, then, is being observant and ready to inspect.

Knowledge: The critical thinker possesses knowledge of the methods of logical inquiry and reasoning. She or he understands how to approach his or her own or another person's argument systematically and with established criteria.

Skills: The critical thinker knows how and when to apply her or his knowledge and does so skillfully.

The Critical Thinker

- Pays attention
- Considers the argument
- Challenges assumptions (including his or her own)
- Asks questions
- Recognizes claims and facts
- Examines the evidence
- Understands the difference between reason and faulty reasoning

Note that when we talk about critical thinking, there are two frequently misconstrued terms. First, the word *critical* often connotes "judging harshly," as in "Hannah was so critical of the restaurant that we couldn't even mention it in her presence." But a critical thinker will think critically about everything, whether he or she loves, hates, or feels neutral about it. Second, the word *argument* often connotes disagreement, especially a verbal disagreement. *Argument* in the academic sense means "a course of reasoning."

College is the place to hone your critical thinking skills and to master the art of active learning, so if some of this is new you're in the right place!

Learning Styles **Exercises**

1. Consider each of your classes. What types of action, reflection, experience, and abstraction do they incorporate? What can you do to integrate the four modes of learning in each class?

2. Do you consider yourself more of a visual, auditory, or tactile/kinesthetic learner? Which learning strategies have you tried that fit your learning style well? What new learning strategies will you try this term?

3. Take a learning style and/or personality inventory. Your instructor or the college counseling center may recommend one or you can go online and complete one of the inventories mentioned in this chapter.

Visit **www.LifeDuringCommunityCollege.com**
for more resources and exercises.

Memory Skills and Multitasking

CHAPTER 16

Now for a test: In what year did Columbus sail the ocean blue? How many days hath September? What percentage of our brains do we actually use?

The answers are 1492, 30, and 100%.

How did you do? Many people would get the first two correct and the last one wrong. When something is stored in the brain and we can retrieve it easily—through a rhyme or because we have a strong association, for instance—it is an indelible memory. If you answered 10% to the last question you remembered correctly, but remembered a myth. The 10% myth is often repeated in our culture in ads and everyday conversations, and it's usually attributed to an authority, such as Albert Einstein. It's also believable: I must be using only 10% of my brain; otherwise, I would have remembered to turn off the stove/pay the bill/make that appointment. No wonder so many of us have locked it away as a memory. In order to remember that it's a myth we'll have to make a concerted effort to re-learn or "un-learn" our prior knowledge.

Memory is not the same thing as learning. A person who remembers all sorts of facts, dates, and information but does not understand their context, is not knowledgeable. A wise person understands concepts, analyzes and synthesizes ideas, and thinks critically—and knows that learning is not simply accruing bits of information. However, strengthening your memory will help you do well in college, so in this chapter, we will:

- define short-term and long-term memory
- discuss the factors that support building memory
- provide memorization tips and tricks
- discuss multitasking and how it inhibits concentration

Short-term and Long-term Memory

Learning literally changes your brain: It changes the internal structure of neurons and increases the number of synapses between neurons. Memory is the record of the learning process.

Short-term memory is a temporary record. Most people's brains hold only about seven units of information for a few dozen seconds. You can capitalize on your short term memory by "chunking" information. Let's say you need to remember this number: 578206781. The task would exhaust your seven units of storage space unless you "chunk" the digits into groups. In this case, you could divide it into three chunks, like a social security number: 578 20 6781. By chunking the information and repeating it you can stretch the capacity of your short-term memory.

Long-term memory includes memory of recent facts (if you can remember the three questions at the beginning of this section, they are technically in your long-term memory) as well as older, consolidated information. There are three processes involved in establishing a long-term memory: encoding, storage, and retrieval.

1) To encode, you assign meaning to the information. Let's say you wanted to remember the meaning of the word "monopoly." You might encode it by associating the word and its meaning with the board game Monopoly.

> ### Want to know more about the brain, learning, and memory?
>
> Check out the Canadian Institute of Neuroscience, Mental Health, and Addiction's website: *The Brain From Top to Bottom* http://thebrain.mcgill.ca/

You could encode it further by breaking the word into its root meanings: *mono* = "alone" and *pol* = "to sell." You could picture your sister monopolizing a conversation. You could assign it emotional or sensory significance (for example, imagining the word written in a certain color).

2) To store the word, you would review it and its meanings. (In other words, study.) Also, get some sleep. Research suggests that sleep plays a significant role in consolidating information.

3) To retrieve it, you follow the path you laid for yourself through encoding. *Monopoly*, hmm, it's like the board game and it reminds me of a certain company, I can see the word written in big steel-colored letters, I can hear my sister jabbering on and on…Ah! *Monopoly* is to have complete control over something!

Remember the story of Hansel and Gretel, the children who went for a walk in the woods and scattered breadcrumbs behind them so they could find their way home later? Animals ate up their breadcrumbs and they were stuck with a wicked witch in a freaky gingerbread cottage. The moral of the story? Don't encode with breadcrumbs. You want something nice and lasting to help you find your way back to your stored memory.

Some long-term memories don't require deliberate encoding and storing: Your first kiss, a traumatic event, the smell of a favorite place. People can recall in great detail where they were and what they were doing on the morning of September 11th, 2001 because the shock of the events of that morning was so great.

Much of what you read, hear, and view in college, however, won't necessarily be intense. Therefore, you will need to make a concerted effort to learn and remember. Here are four factors that influence memory:

Attentiveness: Concentrate on the information.

Motivation: Decide why you want to remember the information. Sometimes this will come naturally. For example, you've probably forgotten the number we used in the "chunking" explanation earlier in this section because you recognized there was no motivation to remember it. In other cases you'll need to determine the purpose and worth of the information.

Emotional state: Remembering your emotional state when you first took in the information can help retrieve it. Also, some emotional states are more conducive to encoding memories than others. If you're anxious and stressed about finals week you might retain a strong memory of your emotional state but have a hard time remembering the course content you need to master.

Context (sights, sounds, smells, place): Connecting the information to sensation, location, or other contextual clues will help you encode it.

You can improve your ability to remember information by incorporating these factors into your daily practice. Your participation in class, note taking, and regular study habits should all help strengthen your memory retention and learning.

Memorization Tips and Tricks

Once you're motivated to memorize material, try these tips and tricks:

Break it down: Memorize sections at a time. Take in new information piece by piece and rehearse as you go—it's less overwhelming than trying to remember the whole thing at once and it's more likely the content will make more sense when you master it bit by bit.

Organize it: What's most important? Which comes first, which last? Is one person, idea, or event dependent on another? What are the relationships between elements? Drawing a graphic organizer can help you understand the material better and retain it, too.

Practice it: Write it, recite it, work with it. The repetition builds the pathways you need to store the information in your long term memory.

Move it: Kinesthetic practice works for a lot of people. This can range from simply pacing while reading to choreographing memory hooks with facial expressions and body movements. The drawback of this method: Your roommate might think you've gone crazy. The benefits: You remember the information.

Overemphasize it: Too much of a concept or fact is sometimes just enough to retain it. When studying vocabulary, for instance, you could try using your newest words in many more situations than you normally would. ("Oh, thank you! That's so *perspicacious* of you! Do you think he's *perspicacious*? If I were more *perspicacious* I would have noticed that..." OK, OK, you get the point. Because you're *perspicacious*....)

Teach it: One way to ensure you've mastered material is to teach it to somebody else. Put it into your own words. Explain it. Draw it out for someone who is not familiar with the material. Anticipate questions a person might have about the topic and be prepared to answer them.

Use mnemonics. Mnemonics are memory tools that help you encode and retrieve information. Songs ("Fifty, nifty United States..."), rhymes ("I before E except after C..."), acronyms, and imagery are powerful ways to remember. Try including sensations in your imagery.

Test it: You want to recall the information in a variety of situations. Reading a page of notes over and over is not going to help most people retain the information. Flashcards–or other means of splitting questions and answers, terms and definitions–are great for this because they force you to come up with the answer.

Your memory skills support all the other academic skills, so we'll come back to some of the terms and ideas from this section. Before we move on to reading, writing, and the other skills, we need to switch gears, interrupt this topic, take just a second, to talk about...hold on, let me check my phone...multitasking.

The Case Against Multitasking

Memory depends on concentration. Multitasking interrupts concentration. It inhibits learning and productivity. In his book *CrazyBusy*, psychiatrist Dr. Edward Hallowell defines multitasking as "a mythical activity in which people believe they can perform two or more tasks simultaneously."

The word multitasking itself is misleading, as research has consistently found that the brain does not have the capacity for focusing on many things at once. Instead, it switches among tasks. Focus. Switch. Focus. Switch. The result is a loss of focus, loss of productivity and, often, an increase in stress. Frequent multitaskers think they are exceptions, that they somehow have mastered the art of managing multiple tasks and information streams. Brain scans and other tests show otherwise. In an interview on National Public Radio, Professor Earl Miller, a neuroscientist at MIT, said, "Switching from task to task, you think you're actually paying attention to everything around you at the same time. But you're actually not." In fact, those who think they are the best at multitasking are, in Miller's words, "deluding themselves."

In 2005, Dr. Glenn Wilson of the University of London conducted a study for Hewlett-Packard on the effects of multitasking. He found that workers distracted by email and phone calls experience a 10-point drop in IQ points—more than twice the impact of smoking marijuana or losing a night's sleep. It's not a permanent drop, but it's still counterproductive.

What about listening to music while studying? In this case, studies support what some students already knew: the brain can effectively block out or "quiet" white noise and music while focusing on a more challenging task, such as memorizing geologic features or learning a chemistry equation. For many people, background noise stays in the background and doesn't compete with the more demanding stuff at hand.

How to break the multitasking habit:

Become conscious of your multitasking. How often do you check email while writing a paper? How frequently do you respond to interruptions such as texts and phone messages?

Set reasonable goals, e.g., "I will turn off my phone for one hour while I finish this math set."

Make it possible. Remove or limit distractions or, conversely, remove yourself from distracting situations. Roommates, your computer, the refrigerator—you know the worst (or favorite?) interruptions and can figure out ways to avoid them. For instance, some people choose to self-monitor time spent on certain websites; services such as minutesplease.com allow users to set time limits on distracting websites. The ironies of college life! You finally move out of the house and now you're the one seeking parental control websites.

Reward yourself for focusing on one task at a time, e.g., "When I am satisfied I understand these equations I can check my phone."

We realize that some of you are still not convinced. No amount of research or number of brain scans will persuade you that multitasking negatively affects learning and concentration. But there's nothing to lose from trying some of the above tips—and a lot to gain if at least one of them helps you focus and work more productively.

Memory Skills & Multitasking **Exercises**

1. Describe a test you've taken recently that tested your ability to recognize information. How did you study for it? How did you do on it? What are the benefits and drawbacks of these kinds of tests?

2. Now describe a test you've taken recently that tested your ability to recall information. How did you study for it? How did you do on it? What are the benefits and drawbacks of these kinds of tests?

3. With a partner, create an exam for this chapter (or another chapter in this book) that tests students' abilities to recognize or recall information. Switch exams with another pair of students. After all parties have taken an exam and graded it, discuss the process: To what extent did preparing a test help you remember the material? What were the best questions and prompts? Why?

4. Multitasking Log. Challenge yourself: What's the longest you can focus on a single school-related task, such as reading, studying, writing, researching, or working in the lab? The next time you're working on a school-related task, keep track of the number of minutes you spend on task versus the number of minutes you spend off task (checking your phone, getting a snack, picking out the perfect music to accompany your work, etc.) Write 1 – 2 paragraphs that reflect on what you learned about your own multitasking and/or the interruptions you encounter.

Visit **www.LifeDuringCommunityCollege.com**
for more resources and exercises.

Time Management

CHAPTER 17

"Time is what we want most, but what we use worst," declared William Penn, who managed to make time to found a colony. We can only speculate what he might have gotten accomplished if he had had a smartphone. (Maybe he'd have been even more efficient? Or maybe he'd have spent his hours browsing reddit?)

As a first-year college student you probably have more free time—that is, time you can plan and define for yourself—than ever. On the other hand, with a challenging class load, work demands (possibly), and social distractions (certainly), it's easy to feel like there aren't enough hours to do what you want to do.

This chapter aims to challenge Penn's statement. Time *is* what we want most—and what we *can* use well. In the following pages, we'll:

- show you how to create a time log

- recommend time management strategies that will help you take control of your time

- reveal common time zappers—and how to avoid them

Your Personal Time Log

In order to manage your time well, you need to know how you currently spend it. Keep track of how you use time for three days—from how long you spend in the shower each day to how many hours you watch television to how many hours you spend sleeping, eating, studying, attending class....You get the picture.

Keep a small notebook with you so you can write things down as you do them, or use a time tracking app, such as ATracker for Apple or Jiffy for Android. Record your activities accurately. (If you're supposed to be studying, but you take a break to check your favorite blog, note it!) It might seem crazy to take 15 seconds to write down that you just checked your feed, but those little tasks add up. All of this data will help you reflect on how you currently spend your time—and, more importantly, help you manage your time realistically and efficiently.

Example of one student's time log:

Time	Activity
8:00 – 8:30 a.m.	Wake up, shower, dress
8:30 – 8:45 a.m.	Check news
8:45– 9:10 a.m.	Eat breakfast
9.10 – 10.15a.m.	Study

Time Management Strategies

Once you have a sense of how you spend your days, it's time to adjust so that you can get the most out of them.

Apps for Time Management

- **Things** (iPhone, iPad, iPod touch)
- **Checklist Wrangler** (iPhone, iPad, iPod touch)
- **ToodleDo** (Android, BlackBerry, iPhone, iPad, iPod touch)
- **Awesome Note** (iPhone, iPad)
- **A+ TimeTable** (Android)
- **myHomework** (Kindle Fire, Android, iPhone, iPad)

1. Create a Term Calendar

This calendar serves as a quick reference to all the major events of the term: Exams, assignments, club meetings, family events, appointments, personal projects, visits from friends or family, etc.

Use the right calendar. Your term calendar can be in any form, but it has to be easy to read and use.

Use your syllabi to write in all important due dates, deadlines, and exams.

Review your term calendar regularly—at least once a week.

Resolve conflicts immediately. Even if the conflicts are weeks or months away, it's best to resolve them as soon as you recognize there's a problem.

2. Create a Weekly Schedule

Map out a rough plan for each week on Sunday or Monday. Block out time for all the things you need and want to do. This takes some time but it will save you energy as the week progresses.

Write in all must-dos, such as class, meetings, and appointments.

Review your term calendar to make sure you don't overlook any deadlines, commitments, or engagements.

Write in some want-to-dos. Schedule time to exercise, meet up with friends, and to do other things that are important to your well-being.

Don't overschedule yourself. Avoid filling up your calendar with every little detail. You want a calendar you can actually live with.

Schedules and to-do lists save energy: You won't have to make as many decisions throughout the day if you've got a lot of them mapped out already.

Sample Weekly Schedule

	Monday	Tuesday	Wednesday	Thursday	Friday
6:30					
7:00					
7:30					
8:00					
8:30					
9:00	Psych 101		Psych 101	Study	Psych 101
9:30					
10:00					
10:30					Study
11:00	Eng Comp	Eng Comp	Eng Comp	Eng Comp	
11:30					
12:00					
12:30			Run w/ Tom		
1:00		Lunch w/Kris			Lunch
1:30					
2:00	Poly Sci	Poly Sci		Poly Sci	Poly Sci
2:30					
3:00			Orientation		
3:30	Workout	Workout			
4:00				Appt. w/ tutor	
4:30				Study	
5:00	Study	Study			
5:30			Span. Club mtg		
6:00					
6:30					
7:00	Dinner	Dinner		Dinner	
7:30					
8:00			Movie @ Kane		
8:30					
9:00		Volleyball		Volleyball	
9:30					
10:00					
10:30					
11:00					
11:30					
12:00					

3. Create Daily To-Do Lists

The to-do list is not just a goal-setting tool; it can also help you relax. After all, it takes energy to maintain a mental record of what you need and want to do. If everything's in your head, you have to remember things, re-remember them (Now what was I going to do after lunch?), wonder if you've forgotten anything, etc. Apps like Todoist and Wanderlist are great for organizing your tasks. No matter what the form, here's how to creat a good to do list:

Refer to your weekly schedule as a starting point. List any appointments, tasks, or activities.

Create a realistic list. Recognize your limitations so you don't go to bed each night feeling like you didn't get anything accomplished.

Time Management Tips

- Set goals and congratulate yourself when you've met them.
- Don't overschedule yourself or overitemize your calendar.
- Break down big tasks into a series of manageable smaller ones.
- Prioritize tasks.
- Do one thing at a time.
- Take action. Get started on major tasks right away.
- Be flexible. Make adjustments as necessary.

Break larger tasks down into smaller chunks. For example, instead of writing "research paper" or even "begin research paper," write "determine topic for research paper." The University of Minnesota has a cool assignment calculator on its website that can assist this process (**www.lib.umn.edu/help/calculator/**).

Prioritize. An assignment due the following day should get higher priority than something due the next week. An especially challenging task should be allotted more time than those that you can whip through.

Cross off as you go. It's important to see that you've completed what you set out to do. Doing so will keep stress at bay.

Transfer tasks. If you don't get something done, transfer it to the next day's list. If it's truly not a priority it might take a few days to get to it.

Common Time Zappers

The big bad twins of time wasting are procrastination and interruptions.

Procrastination can be a beautiful thing. It has caused late-night junk drawer cleaning and encouraged friends to linger over a dinner conversation long after the food has gone cold. Procrastination can be creative ("I know! I'll take up knitting!") or mundane ("Hmm, now how about this font? Or this one?"). But it can catch up in a bad way. You know it has hit if you're finishing a paper at 7:45 a.m. for an 8:00 a.m. class, or if you're fanning your project to dry the glue on your way to turn it in.

If you tend to put things off, take some time to reflect on *why* you procrastinate.

Is it because the assignment seems overwhelming? Is the work difficult to understand? Are there too many distractions? Is procrastination simply a habit? What do you get out of procrastinating? What would be the benefits of not procrastinating? No advice book is effective on its own. However, if you think about your work habits and determine that putting things off increases your stress level, here are some tips to avoid procrastinating:

Create a realistic schedule for completing tasks.

Maintain a positive, motivated attitude towards your work.

Break tasks and projects into manageable blocks, with realistic breaks built in.

Reward yourself for a job well done—and give yourself something to look forward to.

Enlist support. Set goals with a friend so you can help keep each other on track.

Interruptions are the other common time zappers. The world is full of potential interruptions; the trick is to manage them. Here's how:

Just say no. Or at least, just say "later." People will stop by or call and invite you to join them for a meal, a game, a conversation, everything. Get in the habit of letting people know you're busy and telling them when you will be available.

Turn off the phone, TV, computers, etc. If you can't turn the computer off because you need it for schoolwork, make a commitment to ignore the temptations it contains. Every little beep, ping, and ring will distract you from your task and, ultimately, it will take a lot longer to finish the work.

Establish a schedule. Set study hours and let friends, roommates, and family know that those times are off limits.

Get organized. Sometimes it's not others who interrupt us, but our own tendencies toward distraction. Make sure that once you sit down to work you won't be getting up in five minutes to check on something or retrieve something you forgot you need for the assignment.

See Chapter 16 for more information about the effects of interruptions and multitasking, and tips for how to stay focused.

Time Management **Exercises**

1. Keep track of the way you spend your time for three days. Use the sample time log illustrated at the beginning of this chapter, or create one that works well for you. If you really want to see where your time goes, take the data from your three-day log and create a chart. Here's an example:

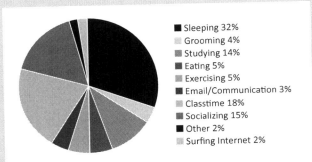

■ Sleeping 32%
▨ Grooming 4%
▨ Studying 14%
■ Eating 5%
▨ Exercising 5%
■ Email/Communication 3%
▨ Classtime 18%
▨ Socializing 15%
■ Other 2%
▨ Surfing Internet 2%

To make your own pie chart, use Microsoft Excel or a free online graphing service like chartgo.com.

2. Create a term calendar and a weekly time schedule. Commit to writing daily to-do lists for this week. At the end of the week, review your term calendar and weekly time schedule. What aspects of this exercise were helpful and something you can imagine continuing for the next month? What aspects of this exercise were not helpful?

3. What are **your** most common "time zappers"? Write down your top five common "time zappers" and devise a plan to limit the amount of time they take up this week. Make sure you set reasonable expectations for yourself! There's no need to avoid your favorite social media site altogether, for example. Just try spending half the time on it that you usually do. Share your goals with a classmate or friend and report to that same person at the end of the week.

Visit **www.LifeDuringCommunityCollege.com**
for more resources and exercises.

Communication, Note Taking, and Study Skills

CHAPTER 18

It's not what you know that's important, but how you know it and how well you communicate it to others. Whether you're majoring in Business Management or Nursing, you need to master the same essential skills: How to learn and how to communicate. The best students (and graduates, for that matter) can write and present well. They participate in class, take good notes, and study effectively. This chapter will help you become not just a successful student, but a master student. It will:

- outline the critical reading, writing, and speaking skills

- explain the importance of participation and give you strategies for participating in a meaningful way

- provide essential tips for note taking and studying

- identify resources that will help you master your studies

Writing Skills

Professors have observed a steady decline in college students' basic writing skills. All students—including math and science majors—need to know how to write well in a variety of contexts. If a student hasn't mastered the basics before college, he or she should seek remediation even before he or she unpacks the new mini-fridge. Colleges usually provide entry-level composition classes, workshops and specialized sessions on writing, in addition to well-staffed writing centers. Some schools, like Purdue University, have top-notch online writing resources—which can be particularly helpful if you're working on a paper at 3 a.m., when no tutoring centers are open. You can help yourself by taking advantage of these resources and learning the essentials of good writing.

> *I never write* Metropolis *for seven cents because I can get the same price for* city.
> *I never write* policeman *because I can get the same money for* cop.
>
> **Mark Twain,**
> **American author and humorist**

Whether you're writing for a science class or an English class, good writing has clarity, focus, voice, fluency, and follows the rules of standard conventions.

Clarity

Be clear and specific. Use precise language, not overblown verbiage or filler material. Edit out any ambiguities or awkward sections.

To check for clarity:

- **Take a break.** Come back to your paper with fresh eyes.

- **Read it aloud.** Listen to the meaning and rhythm of each sentence, as well as to the way the sentences work together.

- **Make sure the style is consistent.** Common inconsistencies include shifting verb tenses and nouns/pronouns (*people* shifts to *a person* or *one* or *everybody* or *you*)

- **Don't use jargon.** Avoid vocabulary words you don't fully understand or don't need.

- **Kill the filler.** Read the paper again, this time looking for fluff or filler material. Frequent fillers: adverbs (Examples: *It was a(n) incredibly rich experience. I sincerely hope you'll respond.*); redundancies (*At this point in time.... It was a very unique opportunity*); and general wordiness (*Seeing as though she was wanting a change....* or *Despite the fact that Harriet was wanting a change for the better...* becomes, simply, *Harriet wanted a change.*)

Focus

Your reader should be able to follow your thoughts from a compelling introduction, through logically organized ideas in the body paragraphs, to a resounding conclusion. Hypothetically, a reader should be able to pick up random sections of your essay and piece them back together in the correct order. How? Because the argument will flow from one idea to the next, you'll have used transition words to signal shifts in ideas or topics, and there will be nothing extraneous to distract from your ideas. Another, more likely, test is if another classmate or your professor could read your paper, then easily respond to the questions, "What is this paper about? What are the author's main ideas?"

To check for focus:

- **Take a break**. Come back to your paper with fresh eyes.

- **Check your thesis statement**. Is it clear, specific, and arguable? Do the ideas in the rest of the paper spring from it?

- **Identify the main idea in each paragraph**. This is usually the topic sentence. Each sentence in the paragraph should connect in some way to the topic sentence. If a sentence doesn't connect, it needs to go, no matter how attached you are to it.

- **Ensure each paragraph is distinct**. If you find yourself restating ideas and even quoting the same material in different paragraphs, that's a sign that you need to pull all of that related material into the same paragraph and cut the rest.

- **Ask a friend to review your paper**. If your friend can restate your thesis and main ideas, you've succeeded. If your friend is confused by parts of it, go back to the paper and rework it until it will pass this test.

Voice

Or, more appropriately, control of voice. Know your audience, purpose, and topic, and write accordingly. Your voice will vary depending on your audience and purpose. The tone you take should be intentional and effective.

To check for voice:

- **Reread the paper out loud**. Ask yourself, *Is there a clear audience, purpose, and topic?* and *Is the tone consistent and appropriate to the audience, purpose, and topic?*

Fluency

You want your reader, whether it's a professor, a teaching assistant, or a classmate, to pause only to reflect on your insights and ideas. You want them to think, "Ah!" and "Hmm, I hadn't thought of that!" not "What?" or "How much longer must I endure?" Fluency is how the paper flows. It should move naturally from one idea to the next. Your sentence structure and word choice should highlight your ideas, not distract from them.

To check for fluency:

- **Take a break.** Come back to your paper with fresh eyes.

- **Check the introduction and conclusion.** Are they compelling? Clearly connected to the topic explored in your paper?

- **Identify transition words and phrases.** Make sure you smoothly transition between each body paragraph or between sentences within a paragraph.

- **Check for common sentence structure errors**, including run-ons, comma splices, and fragments.

Mastery of Conventions

If you're a phonetic speller or an inveterate comma splicer, now is the time to kick the habit. Conventions should not be noticeable to your reader; if you've mastered them, no one will say, "Wow, excellent use of the semicolon!" Or, "I love how her pronouns always agree with their antecedents!" If you haven't mastered them they will distract from your ideas.

To check for conventions:

- **Give yourself time**. Make sure you have enough time between the paper's final printing and its due date to go over it and look for errors in spelling, punctuation, and grammar.

- **Find fresh eyes**. Ask a friend or tutor at the writing center to proofread your paper.

Now that we've described what the final product should entail, let's talk about how to get there: the writing process. You've probably learned at least a couple of different methods for approaching the writing process. These constructs are helpful, especially when a writer recognizes that there is no one-size-fits-all prescription for writing. The writing process depends on the individual student and the writing task at hand.

One crucial thing to remember before you write any paper: Writing is just a part of the process. Thinking of the ideas, researching and reading, taking notes, deciding what to include and what to exclude, developing an outline, then revising and editing—the work of writing is so much more than putting words on paper. Expect to rewrite. Expect to end up with a different product than you aimed for.

Here's a general overview of the writing process:

1. Pre-write. The tasks: identify an interesting topic, determine the position you'll take in the paper, brainstorm ideas, develop an outline, research, read, and gather evidence. If your instructor has provided a rubric, read over it carefully at this stage of the writing process. Rubrics are designed to give students a clear writing target; in other words, they show you exactly what your instructor will consider when he or she evaluates your paper. If time allows, ask for feedback on your outline from a friend or tutor.

2. Write. The tasks: Develop a thesis statement and draft an introduction, then write the body paragraphs and a conclusion.

3. Revise. The tasks: Review your first draft with a critical eye, revise it, and then proofread it.

Here we'll add a step missing from the popular model of the writing process:

4. Reflect. The tasks: After your instructor returns your paper, reread it and any comments he or she made. Keep a critical distance from your own work so you can fairly appraise its strengths and weaknesses. Use any feedback you get to inform the way you write your next paper.

Some words of advice: **Stay flexible** throughout the process and you'll end up with a better paper. For instance, **expect your thesis to change** and develop as you write. With research papers, expect to keep researching in the latter stages of the writing process. Also, **take notes on your readings and sources** as you go so that you won't have to backtrack or, even worse, get stuck without proper records of your sources.

- **Put content first.** Before you think about visual layout and other style considerations, decide what you want to say, how you want to say it, and what you want your audience to take away from your presentation.

- **Keep it lean.** Get your audience's attention at the very beginning and make sure each subsequent part of the presentation gives them something valuable, whether it's information or entertainment.

- **Keep it clean.** Stay focused on your topic and make sure your visuals add to your presentation without cluttering it. Visuals should support the content, not be the content. If you're tempted to read the text on your PowerPoint to the audience, that's a clue that the slides are too text-heavy.

- **Make visuals visible.** Choose appealing colors and make sure text, images, and charts are large enough for the audience to see easily. Use bullet points and spare text. You want the slides and/or images to emphasize what you say, not take over.

- **Be the presenter.** This seems obvious, but sometimes students will spend weeks creating a presentation, then stand in front of the class on the day of the presentation and let the slides do all the work. Or, some students will back off too much when a co-presenter is speaking and become like one of the audience members.

- **Face your audience.** Make eye contact with people in all sections of the room, not just the instructor. If you need to write on your flip chart or smart board during your presentation, pause and then resume speaking.

- **Practice.** Practice your delivery and practice with any technology you're using so you'll feel confident on the day of the presentation.

Presentations ultimately depend on knowledge and preparation. No number of quirky slide transitions or funny YouTube clips can cover weak content.

The process of organizing a presentation with a group usually takes longer and involves more discussion of each step; however, the collaboration can be fruitful if the group members are committed to doing a good job. If you are assigned a group presentation project, try to meet up with your group members as soon as possible so you can map out a plan and preparation schedule that allows all group members to participate fully.

Often, instructors will assign group projects that include a presentation component. In such cases, the presentation is usually worth a big percentage of the overall grade, yet groups often fail to plan well for it. Make sure that you and your group members spend an adequate amount of time preparing for presentations.

Prepared speeches are usually the most formal (and, for some students, the most anxiety-producing) of the three types of public speaking, though some professors will require extemporaneous (spur of the moment) speeches. Here are some tips for writing and presenting a speech:

- **Define your audience and purpose.** An oral presentation needs to be laser-beam focused in order to keep your audience engaged.

- **Prepare your message.** You'll need to start with a good hook, some compelling anecdote, question, statement, or even a joke that engages your audience right away. Decide on your main points and choose the best evidence to support those points. Decide to what extent you want to appeal to your audience's emotions or logic. Make sure your conclusion is clear and effective.

- **Edit.** Once you have a draft, read it out loud at a good public speaking pace several times to hear the rhythm and the message. Read it to a friend and ask him or her to reflect what he or she hears: Are the main points clearly stated? Are transitions between ideas easy to follow? Edit based on any feedback you get.

- **Practice.** Read aloud, first with the entire text in front of you, but later with just those notes you'll have on the day of the actual speech. If you can, film yourself so you can watch your delivery and make changes as needed. Watching yourself on film might not be the most enjoyable way to spend an afternoon, but it will definitely make you aware of any quirks that need to change.

- **Know the rules of good delivery.** Speak loudly and clearly enough to be heard in all corners of the room. Vary your speaking rate (pace), pitch, and volume to keep your audience engaged and to emphasize certain points. Use pauses. Avoid verbal clutter, such as "um" and "like." Practice making purposeful physical gestures that underscore your message. Make eye contact with audience members—not just the one who'll be grading you!

- **Use visuals and other media effectively.** Use only those parts of the film or audio clip that relate to your message. Make sure visuals are large and clear. Don't allow your media to replace your content.

These tips are just a starting point. Your professors will give you more specific information about what's expected in their classes and in their discipline.

How to Gain Confidence with Public Speaking

See each speech or presentation as an opportunity to improve and to overcome anxiety.

Assume that your audience wants you to do well. They do.

Know your stuff. Understand the content thoroughly, including any charts or graphs you'll share with your audience.

Practice your speech or presentation until it feels smooth, then practice some more. It's especially helpful to do a dry run in the location where you'll be speaking. If you can't access the same classroom or lecture hall, find a room that has similar dimensions so you can get used to the space and your own volume.

Concentrate on the content. Yes, your delivery is important, but your audience is there to hear your message. Focusing on the content while you're in front of the room will help you tune out any distracting or anxiety-producing thoughts you have.

Like public speaking and writing, participation is a skill to develop and master. Participation is a bit different, however, because instructors don't always overtly insist on or evaluate it. But they all value student participation.

When you actively listen and respond to class discussions and lectures, you're not just demonstrating curiosity (which instructors love to see, of course!), you're actually activating your curiosity, which in turn leads to true learning. Finals week will be a lot less stressful if you participate fully in class every day because you'll remember the material better and you'll already understand it.

Here's what good participation looks like:

Be prepared. An OK student does the assigned work on time. A good participant completes the assigned work (and suggested readings, whenever possible) and writes down questions she or he has about the material, or connections between the material and something else the class has studied. These notes may become in-class questions or comments.

Be there. Attend class regularly and on time and make it your focus for the hour or however long it lasts. Limit distractions for yourself. Turn off your phone and commit to using your laptop for notes only.

Sit in the "teacher's T"—the front row or middle section of seats—where your instructor will notice you and where you'll be more likely to stay engaged in the lecture or discussion.

Listen well. A good participant tracks the discussion and takes some notes on other students' questions and comments, as well as his own ideas and questions. Note taking during discussion helps you stay focused and interested. It also comes in handy when you're ready to speak because you'll be able to refer specifically to what others have said. You'll also have something to say.

Add to class discussions. Ideally, every student should add to a discussion; that's what makes a vibrant, interesting class. The ideal is not always reality, however. Sometimes classes are too big and the time too short to allow for everyone to have a voice. More often, a few students are superstar participants—or dominators—and the rest stay quiet, unwilling to break into the discussion. If you are the type to hold back, set some goals for participation so that you don't lose out on the learning opportunity. Even a goal of speaking once every other class is better than staying in the background for the term. If you are the type to speak up a lot, see what you can do to help balance the class discussions. You might need to hold back sometimes in order to let others add their voices. Or, you could try asking questions of other students to elicit their opinions on a subject.

Ask questions. Pursue your curiosity and interest. Also, ask questions of other students to facilitate a dynamic class discussion. As we mentioned in Chapter 5, it's best to avoid asking certain questions, such as "Is this going to be on the exam?" and "Did I miss anything?" In general, instructors want to engage students in learning, not simply to inform students how to perform for a grade.

Participate online. Many instructors require that students participate on listservs or online discussion groups. Such forums provide a great opportunity to those students who are shy or who need more time to formulate their ideas and questions. Your online participation should demonstrate insight, attention to detail, and true interaction with the other individuals involved in the discussion. Some students simply dash off their responses and comments online—and miss the opportunity for meaningful interaction, as well as a chance to improve their grade.

Participation is good for your learning and good for your grade. It's also one thing that can make or break a class. You could have the most engaging, interested professor doing academic cartwheels at the front of the room, but all of her or his efforts are for nothing if the students in class don't bring their own engaging, interested selves.

Note Taking Skills

This is one area that tends to separate the college student from the high school student in a big way. High school lecture classes are for good reason broader, slower, and more supportive than college lecture classes. Do you remember a high school teacher ever telling a student to take out her notes? Probably twelve times a class period, right? In college a professor is unlikely to remind anybody to do anything. Unlike high school teachers, college instructors are teaching adults who are paying a lot of money to attend classes. They assume their students know how to take notes and will do so if they're interested in doing well in class.

Of course you are interested in doing well. However, many first-year college students need tips on how to take notes effectively at the college level. Here are the basics you'll need to get started:

Why take notes?

It's possible to go through some classes without taking notes, but we wouldn't recommend it. The instructor or other students might post lecture notes online and instructors often hand out copies of their presentation slides. These are all helpful, but they won't necessarily accomplish the main objective, which is long-term learning. Being in class, actively listening and participating, and taking thoughtful notes will activate your brain and help you encode and store the information and concepts presented that day. Another reason to take good notes is that the printouts you receive do not usually contain all the information and ideas actually conveyed during the class period.

What is note taking?

It is not simply recording a lecture or chapter in writing. When you take notes you decide which ideas are important enough to write down, how they should be organized, and which examples best illustrate them.

What are effective notes?

They identify the main ideas of a lecture or text, identify pertinent supporting details, and are organized and arranged in a way that enhances your understanding of the material at the time and later, when you're studying for the test.

How do you take good notes?

Note taking is a skill and an art. You'll develop your own system eventually. In the meantime, here are four note taking formats to consider:

1. The Formal Outline. This format looks just like you'd expect a formal outline to look: Roman numerals denoting key ideas, other ideas represented by uppercase letters, etc. In essence, you recreate your presenter's outline for her lecture.

2. The Paragraph or List Format. These are similar systems that entail summarizing the key points and supporting details. The list format is distinct because it has more bullet points and indentations to separate information.

3. The Cornell Format. This popular format adds a study helper to the formats listed above. Draw a vertical line about 2 ½ inches from the left edge of your paper: this will be your "cue" column. At the bottom of the page, about 1 ½ inches from the bottom edge, draw a horizontal line: this will be your summary space.

In the right-hand column write your notes as you listen to a lecture or read a text. As soon as you can after class, write in the cue column questions and main ideas that relate to the material in the right-hand column. In the space at the bottom, summarize the notes on that page. The Cornell Format is a great way to review material. The split columns are also a ready-made study guide, as you can easily cover one side up and test yourself.

4. The Mind Map. Some students prefer the mind map method, where a central idea sprouts "branches" of related ideas and details. This enables one to visualize how concepts are related to each other. The mind map is better for notes on texts than lectures.

I Subject Item One

   A. Relevant info or description

   B. More info

II Subject Item Two

   A. Relevant info or description

   C. More info

   D. Etc.

Formal Outline

Write cues here | Main detailed note taking section

Summarize notes here

Cornell Format

Other things to keep in mind about note taking:

Print out lecture slides in advance. Many professors make their lectures available online before the class period. Whenever possible, print out and preview the lecture notes and slides so that you'll be prepared for class. Doing so will also ensure that you don't waste time taking unnecessary notes during class.

Use abbreviations. You can't possibly write everything down—nor should you—but it will help to keep up with your instructor if you use abbreviations whenever possible.

Review your lecture notes soon after class, preferably by the end of the day. Don't wait until the end of the semester to pull them out and study. Reviewing them right away will ensure that you remember the material. Also, you'll be able to see where you have gaps in knowledge—and formulate questions for the instructor the next day.

Keep your notes organized. Title and date your notes and save them in chronological order.

Take notes in your textbook. Write summaries, questions, and ideas in the margins of your text. When you read with a pen at the ready, you interact with the text more and stay focused.

> Effective notes identify the main ideas of a lecture or text, identify pertinent supporting details, are organized and arranged in a way that enhances your understanding of the material, and make studying for the test much easier!

Create a formula and definitions sheet or note cards. This helps you memorize the formulas and definitions in two ways: 1) you get the practice and repetition of writing them out, and 2) you create a handy study sheet you can refer to throughout the semester.

Go light on the highlighter. The problem with highlighting is that it doesn't provide any other information. When you write in the margins of the book you can record your responses and ideas. When you highlight, you simply record lime green color.

You'll probably have a few months of trial and error with note taking before you hit on a system that fits your learning style. Before you know it, though, you'll have your own series of abbreviations and an enviable stock of notes to draw on as you prepare for finals.

The Hard-to-Follow Instructor

Don't give up! If you feel lost after a particularly difficult to understand lecture, **compare notes with classmates, use a recording device** (with permission, of course), **meet with your instructor** to review materials and ask questions, and **ask questions** during the lecture.

Studying

In a way, all the sections that came before this were also about studying. When you take good notes, you are studying. When you actively participate in class, you are studying. When you use the memorization methods discussed in Chapter 16, you are studying.

A narrow view of studying is that it's just for the days before the test. Not so. If you are attentive in each class period and review your notes regularly, you should theoretically get the best sleep of the semester during finals week.

The goal of studying is to own your knowledge—to remember and understand what you've learned—and, of course, to demonstrate that mastery on exams. Here's how:

Create a study plan. As a first-year college student you might have more "free" time than ever before–so it's especially important to learn how to provide structure for that time. Look at your weekly calendar and determine when you'll review notes for each class (we recommend doing so later the same day of the class), when you'll practice skills, when you'll work on assignments, etc. If you break down the work into smaller chunks of time—say, 1 to 2 hours—you'll stay more focused and you'll learn more than if you try to do everything in marathon study sessions. Pace yourself!

Study frequently. Review your notes and readings on a regular basis.

Know what you don't know. After you've reviewed your day's (or week's) notes, identify any holes in your knowledge and figure out who can help you with those missing pieces. You might ask your instructor, a study buddy, or a tutor in the department.

Quiz yourself. Use flashcards, double-sided notes, an app like cram.com, and other means to test your understanding and memory.

Teach someone. If you can explain the material to someone else, you've mastered it.

Collaborate. Study partners and groups are an excellent way to further understanding of material. They can teach you, you can teach them, and together you can figure out ways to remember ideas.

Commit. Effective studying requires concentration and time. Determine your purpose for wanting to do well, then commit to yourself.

Before you get too far into your first year, figure out which study conditions work best for you through a combination of trial and error and self-reflection. Be honest with yourself as you answer the questions on the next page. You might prefer to study in a bustling café filled with attractive people and pastries, but is that the optimum place to work?

Once you've filled out the Personal Study Conditions Inventory, we recommend you keep it handy. You'll have plenty of opportunities to get distracted in college and this inventory might remind you of your personal optimum study conditions.

Personal Study Conditions Inventory

Time

What times of day (or night) do I have the most energy?

When am I most focused?

When do I have the least energy?

When am I least focused?

Place

Where am I likely to maintain focus?

Where am I likely to be most productive?

Where am I likely to be inspired and motivated?

Where am I likely to be distracted and interrupted?

Mode

Do I study best with total quiet or some noise?

Do I study best in solitude or around people?

Do I stay more focused when I have a deadline?

Visit **www.LifeDuringCommunityCollege.com**
for more resources and exercises.

Academic Support Resources

A hallmark of a master student is the ability to seek and obtain assistance. We recommend you get help before you even know you need it. Especially for your first term assignments, you should draw on available resources: do your math homework in the math lab, ask for feedback on your essays from the writing center staff, and get advice on preparing presentations from the staff of the speaking lab. Doing so can only help you—and it might prevent problems.

Potential resources include:

- Your instructor
- Teaching assistants
- Your advisor
- Academic Support Services
- Math, writing, or speaking labs
- Tutoring Center
- Computing Center
- Supplementary Instruction (SI) groups (study groups led by trained educators)
- Online tutoring, labs, and writing resources

Don't fret if your writing skills are a little rusty or if your study habits have been lax in the past. A successful student always seeks improvement, never a perfection that does not exist. Being your own best teacher means challenging yourself, trying new approaches, and sometimes imposing discipline. The skills we discuss in this chapter are vital and well worth the effort it takes to master them.

Communication, Note Taking & Study Skills **Exercises**

1. Try a new routine: If you usually study in your room, try studying in the library. If you usually study in the evening, try doing it in the afternoon. Note the pros and cons of each studying situation.

2. Create a 5-minute individual or group presentation on a topic related to this course. Ideas might include Study Habits, Places to Study, and the Most Valuable Resources on Campus. After your presentation, write a one-page reflection on the presentation's strengths and weaknesses.

3. Reflect on your participation skills: What are your strengths in this area? What are your weaknesses? Give yourself three specific challenges related to participation. How will you assess if you've been successful in meeting these challenges?

4. Try two of the four note-taking formats in one of your other classes this week. Write a reflection (outline form is OK) on which format you think was most effective and why.

Visit **www.LifeDuringCommunityCollege.com**
for more resources and exercises.

Test Taking Strategies

CHAPTER 19

At some point college exams will be a memory, something to reflect on, and even, in some cases, chuckle about. The anxiety will be just part of the past, as will the stacks of 3 x 5 flash cards, the long study sessions, and the smell of freshly sharpened No. 2 pencils.

While some people might consider exams a nightmare designed to weed out the faint of heart, it's important to remember that they exist for good reason. Namely, to consolidate learning. Exams provide an incentive to learn. They also give you a purpose for synthesizing the information and ideas you've encountered in a unit or semester: If you didn't go through the steps of reviewing, studying, and testing you wouldn't know the course content as deeply. Exams also serve as important indicators of gaps in your knowledge; in this way, both you and your instructor learn from your performance on an exam.

Of course, exams are an imperfect measure of what a person truly knows—a well-prepared student can have a bad day and a well-intentioned professor can write a bad test. Knowing that exams are imperfect should help ease any anxiety; if you have a bad day and do poorly on one, it's just that—a bad day and one test—not a marker of your ultimate success or failure.

This chapter will:

- walk you through exam anxiety
- help prepare you for the days before the exam
- offer unique strategies for taking various types of exams
- provide the hows and whys of reviewing a graded exam

> **Focus on the value of learning the information you're being tested on.**

Public Speaking Skills

Public speaking, both informal and formal, is another important part of the college experience. Some might use the term "unavoidable," as the mere thought of speaking in public is a common source of anxiety and fear. If you are one of those people, it might be startling (or humorous) to realize that here you are, paying thousands and thousands of dollars to have instructors insist you do the very thing you most avoid doing. Take the long view: College is supposed to challenge you, and rising to these challenges now will make you feel more confident later, when the stakes are higher. For those of you who like public speaking, here's your opportunity to polish those skills.

Many schools have speaking labs, similar to writing centers. Speaking labs are staffed with people trained to assist students in preparing for public speaking and video presentations. They often offer one-on-one assistance as well as all the necessary equipment and technology.

The public speaking you do will vary depending on your area of study, but most likely will include the following types: Impromptu speaking, presentations, and speeches.

Impromptu speaking is in class and on the spot, hence it is the most informal of the types of public speaking. Your preparation for speaking in these cases will be minimal. That is, you'll have read the material and prepared for class, but you probably won't have speaking notes. Here are some tips for responding to questions and sharing ideas on the spot in class:

- **Listen well.** Your classmates' and instructors' ideas will inform your own. When you listen carefully, you'll be able to add meaningfully to the discussion. Also, you'll be less likely to be caught off guard if your professor calls on you. If your instructor does call on you and you don't fully understand her or his question (or if your attention was wandering), rephrase the question in your own words or ask him or her to repeat it.

- **State your opinion.** In the course of a discussion, your opinion will change and develop, so state your opinion as it is in that moment.

- **Explain your reasoning.** Why do you think the way you do? What evidence supports your opinion? Anticipate these questions and use them to develop your point.

- **Show respect.** Acknowledge the validity of previous speakers even if you disagree with their arguments. Restate what you hear and use "I" statements. Example: "I agree with Travis's point about the Supreme Court's decision. However, I see it from a different angle...."

Presentations, informal and formal, are often required in college classes. To give successful individual or group presentations:

- **Define your audience and purpose.** A persuasive presentation for a small group of faculty and students requires a different style than an entertaining presentation for a group of peers.

Dealing with Test Anxiety

Almost everybody gets the pre-test jitters. In fact, some of that nervousness may help bolster performance. Some students, however, experience intense anxiety. According to Greenberger and Padesky, clinical psychologists and authors of *Mind Over Mood*, "Anxiety can be reduced either by decreasing your perception of danger or increasing your confidence in the ability to cope with threat." When we apply that statement to test taking, we need to ask, "What is the perception of danger?" and, "How does one increase confidence in one's ability to cope?"

We'll let you answer the first question for yourself. Here are some tips for increasing confidence in your abilities:

Give yourself sufficient time to prepare for the exam.

Imagine the test as one step in a process (after all, it is!). Notice how successfully you complete each step (the steps might include attending class, taking notes, creating a study guide, completing practice quizzes, and taking the test).

Schedule an appointment with your instructor at least one week prior to the exam if you have questions about any material that confuses you.

Participate in a study group or prepare with another student.

Visualize yourself succeeding on the exam.

Avoid studying with other students who seem intensely anxious.

You can't avoid exams in college, so you'll have many opportunities to face your fears and build up your confidence. If you have such bad test anxiety that you *do* avoid exams you should make an appointment with your academic advisor and/or a counselor to discuss how your fear is impacting your studies.

Test Anxiety Worksheet

My specific fears related to test taking:

Steps I can take to increase my confidence:

Visit **www.LifeDuringCommunityCollege.com**
for more resources and exercises.

Preparing for an Exam

The biggest mistake students tend to make before an exam is to disrupt their normal schedules. Preparing for an exam in such a way interferes with familiar sleeping, eating, and other habits and makes it difficult to concentrate on the task at hand. Here are some ways to make the most of the night before and the day of an exam:

Maintain a regular diet and sleep schedule. Staying up late and snacking on unhealthy foods can not only diminish your performance on the exam, but also add unneeded stress.

Give yourself sufficient time to gather necessary materials. Doing so will ensure that you have everything you need when you get to the exam and you won't be madly scrambling to get out of your apartment.

Do what you need to do to be alert, whether that's taking a shower, having a real breakfast, or going out for a run.

If allowed, bring a small snack and/or drink into the exam room so that you can maintain energy throughout the test.

Glance through your study materials on the morning of the exam to refresh your memory.

Cramming

No one will recommend cramming for an exam, but if you do find yourself in such a situation, here's the "right" way to cram:

Maintain a positive attitude. If you attended the class and completed your assignments, you should do fine on the exam. Sure, you could do better with more time to study, but you'll do the best you can with the limited time you have left.

Make efficient use of the time you do have. Focus on the concepts and ideas with which you are unfamiliar, rather than reviewing materials you already know well.

Take frequent, short breaks about once an hour to stretch and walk around a little. This will keep you active, alert, and awake.

Study in a location that encourages concentration, such as a desk or table. Avoid studying on your bed, sofa, or anywhere that will be too comfortable and distracting.

Avoid stimulants like coffee, soda, or others that might keep you alert for a time, but leave you in an extremely drowsy or agitated state.

Eat healthy foods while you are studying and immediately prior to the exam.

Try to get sufficient rest so that you can think clearly during the exam.

Strategies for Taking an Exam

Having a game plan to follow on exam day will make the experience less stressful. The following are strategies that should help you through the examination process.

Arrive early. Have your materials ready and find a comfortable seat. In fact, sitting in your regular sit can help you recall information.

Relax and think positively: *I can do this. I know this stuff.*

Dress appropriately. This seems silly, but being too hot or too cold can easily distract you.

Preview the exam. When you receive your exam, take a few minutes to look it over. Make sure you check each page, front and back, so you don't miss a section. This will allow you to determine the amount of time you should spend on each part.

Read the instructions carefully. It takes time to do, but it's critical. There have been countless points lost by not following directions, points lost because students only wrote one essay when two were required, or wrote "T" instead of "True" and got marked down, or failed to write their answers in the required format.

Start with what you know. Some exams questions must be approached in sequence. However, with some exams you can skip around and answer the questions you know first. There are advantages to doing this: it builds confidence, maximizes the number of points you'll earn, and allows you more time later in the test to tackle the really tough questions. Also, answering questions you know immediately might help jog your memory for those that are more difficult.

Write legibly. Instructors can't grade what they can't read. If your instructor has to squint and puzzle through big chunks of your writing, she or he will give up and only give you points for those parts he or she can read. Take the time to write clearly.

Show your work. Leave a record of your thought process so your instructor can see how you arrived at your answer. Sometimes you'll get partial credit for taking the correct steps even if you ended with a wrong answer.

Concentrate. Easier said than done, but try to zero in on your exam, not on the sniffles and coughing coming from your classmates.

Don't panic if you don't know the answer to a question. Skip that question and come back to it after you've answered the ones you know. It's usually best to attempt an answer even if you're pretty sure it will be wrong. You might get partial credit if you can demonstrate some knowledge related to the question.

Learn from the exam as you take it. On many exams, questions build on one another or provide clues for other questions' answers.

Take time at the end of the exam. If possible, give yourself a chance to review your test after you complete it.

Hand in your test on time. Students have received a score of zero for not turning in a test on time. Don't take that risk.

Types of Exams

In this section we'll discuss ways of approaching the most common types of exams you'll encounter: essay, true/false, multiple choice, open book/open note, take-home, and oral exams.

Essay Exams

- Read all questions thoroughly before you begin. Answer questions you feel most comfortable with first.

- Make a quick outline of key points and ideas before you begin writing. This will help prevent the "Oh no! I'm writing my conclusion and I finally know what I want to say!" experience.

- Get to the point. Make your focus clear from the outset of your essay and maintain that focus throughout the body paragraphs.

- Leave extra space between paragraphs and in the margins of your answer, in case you need to add additional information later. (This isn't always possible, as some essay tests have a page limit and you won't be able to afford any blank space.)

- Use specific, relevant details to support your point and prove your understanding of the material. Cite course materials if necessary.

- Use transition words and phrases to signal a shift in ideas. (e.g., "Not only…, but also…" or "Another example is…") These transitions will make your essay smooth and easy to read.

- Write legibly. Your instructor can't grade what he or she can't read.

True/False Exams

- Skim over all the statements before you begin. Answer the statements you know first then return to those you don't know.

- Pay attention to wording. Read the statements very carefully: if any part of the statement is false, you need to mark "False." Some wording, such as the use of double negatives, can be very confusing.

- Watch out for key words or qualifiers such as "all," "most," "sometimes," "never," or "rarely." Although the answer to a statement may appear to be true at first, the addition of one of these key words can change the meaning of the statement and make it false.

Multiple-Choice Exams

- Skim over all the questions before starting the exam and answer those you know the answers to first.

- Anticipate the answer as you read the question, then find the available choice that best matches your answer.

- If you are unsure of the answer to a question, read over all the answers provided. Use the process of elimination to narrow down your choices.

- If there is no penalty for incorrect answers, guess on those questions you don't know. If there is a penalty, it may not be worth it to guess.

Open Book/Open Note Exams

These can be the most difficult tests to take, perhaps because students underestimate them. Here are some tips to help you succeed on this type of exam:

- Study for open book/open note exams just as you would for a closed book one. Many students under prepare because they know they'll have access to their materials.

- Organize your notes and mark your textbook before the exam so you don't spend precious time searching for information.

- Read all the questions first, then answer the ones you know immediately. You may want to confirm you know the answer by checking in your materials, but it's not always necessary.

Watch out! Open book exams are often more difficult than other types of exams.

- Use your materials. Your instructor expects more detail and diligence than he would of a closed book test. Use direct quotes if appropriate, cite sources whenever possible, and include specific details if you have them and they're relevant to your answers.

Take-Home Exams

As with open book/open note exams, many students fail to prepare sufficiently for take-home exams. Here's how to succeed on them:

- Organize all study materials, such as notes, reading, and homework assignments.

- Review the exam thoroughly before you leave the classroom. If you have any questions, ask the instructor. Also, ask if and how the instructor can be contacted if you have additional questions later.

- Do thorough work. Instructors have higher standards for take-home tests than for in-class ones.

- Stay focused. It may be tempting with all of the time you have for the assignment to write more or do additional, unnecessary work. Develop thorough responses to the question(s), but don't waste your time—or your instructor's—with unrelated information.

- Use your materials. Your instructor expects more detail and diligence than she would of a closed book test. Use direct quotes if appropriate, cite sources whenever possible, and include specific details if you have them and they're relevant to your answers.

> Instructors often have higher expectations for take-home exams than in-class exams.

Oral Exams

These tests are more common during graduate school, but you might encounter an oral exam as an undergraduate.

- Prepare materials for the exam just as you would for an essay or other test. Your oral exam answers should have key points and support for those points.

- Make sure you understand the requirements and expectations.

- Practice with another student, if possible.

- Time yourself when you practice if your oral exam will be timed.

- If your instructor allows a few moments to gather your thoughts before you launch into an answer, use that time.

- Be concise and clear with your response. Use signal words to help your listener follow your ideas. ("*Another* piece of evidence that supports my point is…" or "My *second* rationale is…") Avoid rambling.

Check it Twice!

Before you turn in your exam, double check it to make sure you've taken care of the details. Some common mistakes are easily avoidable. Follow these steps every time:

- **Make sure your name, student identification number, and other required information are included on your exam.**

- **Double check the Scantron/bubble form (if applicable) to verify you've filled in the correct bubble for each question.**

- **Review the exam and instructions a final time** to ensure that you have fulfilled all the requirements.

Review Your Graded Exam

You probably won't post your graded exam on the refrigerator, but you definitely should review it. Why? One reason is to check for any mistakes in calculations your instructor or TA might have made. The other, more powerful, reason is to learn from the mistakes you made and the test itself.

These following tips will help you effectively review your exam:

Calculate your score to verify that the grader computed it correctly.

Review the exam for answers that were marked wrong but you still think are correct. Rework the answers, this time with all the resources available to you. If you cannot arrive at the correct answer on your own, ask for assistance from the tutoring center or your instructor.

Analyze the test itself: Where do the questions originate? Lectures? Textbook? Assignments? This will make it easier for you to focus your studying for the next exam for that instructor.

Correct each of the incorrect and partially correct answers to better understand why they were wrong or what they were missing. Sometimes instructors provide model answers to assist students with this process.

Schedule an appointment with your instructor to discuss any questions you may have and to ask for his or her advice on studying for future exams.

Exams are a necessary if not entirely pleasant part of the learning process. Stay focused on your ultimate goal—learning—and you'll be able to diffuse some of the stress exams cause. Approach each class hour and study session with a desire to learn, and tests will become just another step in the process.

Exams **Exercises**

1. What is your standard method for studying for exams? Rate its effectiveness on a scale from 1 to 10, where 1 is least effective and 10 is most effective. Explain your rating.

2. What tips from this chapter are you most likely to try? Why?

3. What style of exam (essay, true/false, multiple-choice, etc.) do you find most difficult? Why?

4. Describe an excellent test you've taken: one that challenged you, truly assessed your knowledge, and taught you something valuable. Discuss with a partner.

5. Read the following statement, then discuss the following questions with a partner or group:

   Students tend to focus too much on the grade associated with an exam and not enough on the value of learning in preparation for it.

   What can instructors and institutions do to help students focus more on the value of learning?

   What can students do to help themselves focus more on the value of learning?

Visit **www.LifeDuringCommunityCollege.com**
for more resources and exercises.

Grades and Your GPA

CHAPTER 20

Good grades open doors. Four year college admissions officers consider overall grade point average (GPA) as well as grades in specific course work. So, too, do future employers. In fact, according to the National Association of Colleges and Employers' Job Outlook 2013 survey, "more than 78 percent [of employers] say that they will screen candidates by GPA." The job market plays a role here: When employers have an abundance of applicants, standards go up. If an employer has a GPA cutoff, it will likely be higher in years of high unemployment.

Good grades aren't the only way to advance. Internship experience and commitment to extracurricular activities are also highly valued. However, it's worth noting how important grades are so that you can take steps now to do well in your classes—and to maintain a solid GPA throughout your college years.

This chapter will:

- provide an overview of grading systems
- outline alternative grading options
- illustrate the value of earning good grades your first year
- recommend strategies to maintain good grades

3.0

Most of the employers who have a GPA cutoff—in other words, who won't consider applicants with less than a certain GPA—report that 3.0 is the magic number. Other criteria include the applicant's college, major, and experience.

Source: NACE Job Outlook 2013 Survey

Grading Systems

Instructors work hard to grade fairly and accurately, but the methods of grading vary widely and may cause confusion for students. Some instructors assess student performance based on one or two major written assignments; others don't grade written work but calculate students' grades based on a test or two per semester. Some instructors grade participation, some offer extra credit assignments, some drop the lowest exam grade. The course syllabus should explain how students are assessed.

Despite the variation in methods and means of grading, there are only two major grading systems that you're likely to encounter:

Absolute Grading

This is the most common grading system. The instructor sets the point or percentage range for each letter grade at the beginning of the term. For example, a score of 90% or above may be predetermined to be an A. Theoretically, with the absolute grading system, every student in class could get an A on a given test.

Relative Grading

Also known as "grading on a curve." This is a more competitive grading system, as each student's performance is evaluated against her peers. There are many ways to curve grades. Here's one example: Let's say the average score in the class is a 79%. If the instructor uses a standard deviation calculation to determine the cutoffs for each grade, an 89-100% is an A, 85-88% is a B, 72-84% is a C, 60-71% is a D, and 59% or below is a failing grade.

Make sure you review your course syllabi and understand within the first week of school the process and system that each of your instructors uses. If the grading criteria are unclear, ask your instructor to clarify.

Grading Options

There are alternatives to receiving a letter grade for a class.

Pass/Fail

Many colleges allow some variation of the Pass/Fail option, though it's usually available only for non-required courses or electives. This is a great alternative for students interested in taking a certain class who want to limit the stress of working for a grade. Some schools encourage students to pursue curiosity and passion by taking interesting classes outside of their department, using the Pass/Fail option. For example, a History major fascinated by Physics might elect to take a Physics class Pass/Fail. Usually, your instructor will not know you are taking the course as a Pass/Fail. He or she will submit your grade to the registrar, who will convert it to a P or F on your transcript.

Incomplete

The incomplete is a good option for students who have experienced a major event or illness that has interfered with their ability to complete coursework. A student who is interested in pursuing this alternative needs to discuss it with his or her instructor and get permission. Usually, the student and instructor will then agree on a completion date that is sometime after the actual end of the course. An "Incomplete" will appear on the student's transcript until the completion date. The student needs to submit all work and take all exams by that completion date in order to earn a letter grade for the course. A missed deadline may result in an F.

Withdrawal

There is a window of time after the term begins when a student can add or drop a course without the change affecting his transcript. This allows students to attend classes for the first few meetings and make an informed decision to stay in a class, switch to another class, or drop the class altogether. If a student withdraws after a certain date, however, a W will appear on his or her transcript.

Challenging Your Grade

Even college instructors make mistakes. You may find that an exam or assignment has been graded incorrectly. You may think that a question was worded awkwardly, which led you to answer it incorrectly. Or you may feel an instructor has treated you and your work unfairly. If any of these situations occur,

Gather the information you need to make your case. Refer to class notes, textbooks, previous assignments, and tests.

Make an appointment to discuss your concerns with your instructor.

Avoid defensiveness and anger. Listen to your instructor's reasoning carefully so you fully understand the situation.

If you are still not satisfied after meeting with your instructor, make an appointment to discuss your concerns with your academic advisor and ask for her or his advice. Your student handbook will also outline the steps for challenging a grade.

If you are still not satisfied, you can petition to have the grade changed through the department committee that oversees the course or through the formal process outlined in your Student Handbook or College Catalog.

The Value of Starting Strong

It's a lot easier to start off with a good grade point average than to dig out of a hole later. If you start strong and keep the momentum going, you won't have to worry so much about your grade slipping when you're in the really challenging classes your last two years of college. Here's an illustration that tracks the progress of two hypothetical students, Alex and Pat.

As you can see, Alex did poorly the first term and well the second term. However, Alex has a long way to go to raise his cumulative GPA and his classes will only get more difficult.

Starting college with good grades is like an insurance policy: it protects you from potential GPA damage if you get a lower grade later in your college career.

First Term	Alex	Pat
Chemistry *(4 credit hours)*	C	A
Anthropology *(3 credit hours)*	B	A
Creative Writing *(4 credit hours)*	C	A
Calculus *(4 credit hours)*	B	A
Grade Point Average	**2.47**	**4.0**

Second Term	Alex	Pat
Chemistry II *(4 credit hours)*	B	B
Art History *(3 credit hours)*	A	B
Biology *(4 credit hours)*	A	B
Calculus II *(4 credit hours)*	A	A
Grade Point Average	**3.73**	**3.27**

Cumulative Grade Point Average	**3.10**	**3.63**

Strategies for Maintaining Good Grades

Well, you could sign up for the easiest courses and take the bare minimum number of credits necessary to maintain enrollment and/or financial aid. It wouldn't be very rewarding, though. Here's how to challenge yourself, get an excellent education, *and* maintain good grades:

DO:

Focus on learning. Attend class, study, and complete course work. When you master the material, the grades will show it.

Balance your course load. Take a reasonable number of classes, and balance very challenging classes with not-so-difficult ones.

Make sure you understand the objectives of the course and how you'll be evaluated.

Connect with your instructors. Get comfortable with asking questions and asking for assistance. Discuss any concerns you have with your instructor. If you feel an error has been made, bring it to your instructor's attention.

DON'T:

Lose focus as you enjoy your college freedom. First-year grades do matter and they can be hard to make up for later.

Overload yourself with too many challenging classes in the same term.

Give up. Any improvement you make in your grades—either in a specific course during a term or in your overall grade point average—will help and is worth the effort.

Get defensive or angry if you disagree with a grade you have received. Become familiar with how your college handles these kinds of situations and participate in the process.

Grades Exercises

1. Review the syllabi of the classes you're enrolled in this term. What are the grading procedures of each instructor?

2. Research alternative grading options available at your college and the requirements for electing those alternatives.

Visit **www.LifeDuringCommunityCollege.com**
for more resources and exercises.

Paying for College

Depending on your COA, your FAFSA, your EFC (which will be noted on your SAR), and your enrollment status, you may qualify for a FSEOG or a Pell or your parents may get a PLUS. Now, your FAA can tell you all about how your aid is disbursed, how interest will accrue, and if it is capitalized. For more information, check out the NSLDS.

Sometimes it feels like you need a degree just to figure out how to pay for college. Or two degrees: one in finance and one in acronyms. To make matters more confusing, the rules and amounts seem to change daily.

In this chapter we will explain the most critical terms related to college finance, give you an overview of your options for paying for this investment that is your college education, and provide you with the websites and phone numbers that will be essential for figuring out your personal college financing plan. Here are the sections included in this chapter:

- Work
- FAFSA
- Federal Grants and Work-Study
- Loans
- Other options

Work

While going to school full time and working is a challenge, it is not uncommon. In fact, nearly 39% of full-time college students work (Source: **www.bls.gov**). The benefits to working while attending school are:

- a reduced debt load when you graduate
- work experience that can help you qualify for future internships and jobs
- experience managing time and balancing priorities

The drawbacks to working while in school are:

- extra stress from trying to budget time and energy
- lack of focus on academics might mean less success in your classes
- little time for social or extracurricular activities

Even if you do decide to work while taking classes, you'll probably need to supplement your income with other sources. For many students, that means turning to Uncle Sam or private organizations for scholarships, grants, and loans.

29.6

(the average number of hours undergraduate students work* per week) *includes work-study, assistantships, and traineeships. Source: US Dept. of Education Profile of Undergraduate Students, Sept. 2010. http://nces.ed.gov/

The FAFSA

Completing the Free Application for Federal Student Aid (FAFSA) is a kind of rite of passage—for the student and, usually, his or her parents. As its name states, the application is free. It's also necessary if you want to be considered for the majority of financial aid options. Applications are accepted as early as January 1st and as late as the end of June, but you want to submit yours as soon as possible in order to have the best chance of receiving financial aid. Go to **www.fafsa.ed.gov** to complete yours online. Contact the Federal Student Aid Information Center at 1-800-4-FED-AID with questions you have about the form and/or the process.

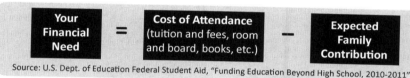

| Your Financial Need | = | Cost of Attendance (tuition and fees, room and board, books, etc.) | − | Expected Family Contribution |

Source: U.S. Dept. of Education Federal Student Aid, "Funding Education Beyond High School, 2010-2011"

After you complete your FAFSA, you will receive a Student Aid Report (SAR) that details your family's expected contributions to your college costs. Your eligibility for financial aid—and for different types of financial aid—will be determined based on this information.

A Guide to Financial Aid Acronyms

COA: Cost of Attendance
FAFSA: Free Application for Federal Student Aid
EFC: Expected Family Contribution
SAR: Student Aid Report
FSEOG: Federal Student Educational Opportunity Grant
FAA: Financial Aid Administrator
NSLDS: National Student Loan Data System
EEK: The sound a student makes when he or she sees the total cost of textbooks for the semester

Federal Grants and Work-Study

Many schools participate in federal programs that offer aid in the form of federal grants and work study opportunities. Remember, you may be competing with other students for these grants and work study jobs, so fill out any required paperwork—including the FAFSA—as early as possible!

Federal Pell Grant: Students who demonstrate financial need may qualify for a Pell Grant. Pell Grants, which may be as large as $5,775, do not have to be repaid. If you are awarded a Pell Grant, your school may disburse the money to you directly or credit your account.

Federal Supplemental Educational Opportunity Grant: If you are awarded a Federal Supplemental Educational Opportunity Grant (FSEOG), you may receive up to $4,000 a year. The money will be disbursed to you by your college. You may receive checks or a credit to your account. You do not have to repay a FSEOG.

Bookmark these sites!

studentaid.ed.gov
www.fafsa.ed.gov

The world of financial aid can be confusing and it changes quickly. These websites have clear, up-to-date information.

Federal Work Study: If you qualify for a work study program, you will be eligible for a job either on campus or with another organization that has an agreement with your college. You will be paid monthly wages by the college.

Teacher Education Assistance for College and Higher Education (TEACH) Grant: You may be eligible for up to $4,000 per year if you are enrolled in a teacher education program and agree to teach for a period of time in a high-need field or in a high-need school. If you complete your teacher education program but do not fulfill your contract agreements, you must repay the TEACH grant. Note: Select schools offer this grant. Check with your Financial Aid department to find out if your school offers this opportunity.

Iraq and Afghanistan Service Grant: If your parent or guardian died serving in the military in Iraq or Afghanistan, you may be eligible for a federal grant up to $5,500.

Federally Funded Loans

There are a variety of loan options available to students and their parents. The following are the federally funded loan options:

Federal Perkins loans: Perkins loans are low-interest loans for students with exceptional financial needs. The U.S. Department of Education allots a certain amount to participating colleges, which determine the students with the greatest needs. Your college will either disburse Perkins money directly to you or it will credit your account. There are no fees for Perkins loans.

Subsidized (also known as the Federal Direct Stafford/Ford Loan): If the Department of Education determines that you have financial need, you may qualify for a subsidized loan, which means you will not be charged interest on the amount you borrow while you are enrolled (at least half time) in school. You will also get an interest-free grace period for the 6 months after you graduate, drop out, or drop below the minimum number of enrollment credits. If you apply for and receive a deferment after the grace period expires, you will not be charged interest while your loan is deferred.

Unsubsidized (also known as the Federal Direct Unsubsidized Stafford/Ford Loan): Same as above except Uncle Sam does not pay the interest on your loan while you're in school. You can wait to make payments until after you graduate, but the interest on your loan will accrue and be added to the total amount you owe when you do start making payments.

PLUS loans: If you are still considered a dependent, your parents may apply for a federal PLUS loan to cover part of the cost of your education. PLUS loans are not based on financial need. To be eligible for a PLUS loan, the student must be enrolled in school more than half time and the parents must have a good credit history. Unlike the Stafford/Ford loans, parents are responsible for repaying PLUS loans. If you go on to graduate school, you may be eligible to apply for and receive a PLUS loan on your own behalf.

Private Student Loans

Private student loans are another option. Unlike the loans described in the above section, private student loans are funded by private institutions, such as banks and credit unions. While these loans are readily available for many borrowers, they carry more risk than those loans funded by the federal government. A private student loan may:

- have a very high interest rate. We have seen rates as high as 18% for private student loans.

- have a variable interest rate. That means your monthly payment amount may change unexpectedly.

- require that you begin repaying while you're still in school.

- not offer loan forgiveness or forbearance.

- have a prepayment fee or penalty fees.

A word of caution: Take your time to review all the options available to you. If you take out a loan it could be with you for many, many years. Spend some time calculating how long it will take you to repay the loans you take out (a simple financial aid calculator is available at **www.finaid.org**).

Other Options

There are many ways to piece together the funds you need to pay for your education. Here are some routes students take to make their college dream a reality:

According to the Consumer Financial Protection Bureau, "Ten percent of recent graduates of four-year colleges have monthly payments for all education loans in excess of 25% of their income." Source: CFPB Report on Private Student Loans, 2012. **Consumerfinance.gov**

State and local aid: Your state and local organizations may offer grants and scholarships. Go to the US Department of Education's Education Resource Organizations Directory website for all the links you need to find out about what aid your state and other organizations may have available.

Service: Students who serve in programs such as AmeriCorps may receive compensation and other benefits that will pay for some or all of their college costs or loans. Serving in the military is another route to paying for one's education.

Scholarships: There are innumerable scholarships available to students—the key is to know where to look for them. Your parents' employers may have scholarships available, or the local Rotary Club, your bank or credit union, an organization that focuses on your proposed area of study…. Ask around, check your school's financial aid office, and use the Internet to search for scholarship and grant money.

Competitive or conditional grants: At **http://studentaid.ed.gov** you can find a list of grants for students with exceptional skills or who agree to "pay off" the grant with a term of service. For example, the TEACH Grant Program gives students money if they agree to teach for a certain amount of time in high-needs areas of the country. The Academic Competitiveness Grant is available to students who have proven themselves in a rigorous course of study.

Paying for College Exercises

1. Do you think students should have free or low-cost education available to them if they prove themselves academically in high school? Why or why not?

2. Visit the websites on page 154 and explore the resources, tools, and documents that pertain to your financial situation. What are the top 5 most helpful sections of these pages?

3. Make a list of organizations you and your parents belong to, interests you have, and subjects you would like to study. Search the U.S. Department of Education's Education Resource Organizations Directory website and/or your college's financial aid office for scholarship and grant opportunities that might be available to you based on your list.

4. Create a calendar for the upcoming year that will help you organize the various scholarship and aid deadlines.

Visit **www.LifeDuringCommunityCollege.com**
for more resources and exercises.

Budgeting Made Easy

CHAPTER 22

"That's not in my budget" and "We're living on a budget." The word *budget* might bring to mind restrictions and limitations, a list of shouldn'ts and can'ts. But a budget is simply a plan. Any limitations it involves are actually steps on the way to a goal.

Budgeting when you're in college might seem unnecessary. After all, when you're broke, you're broke, right? What's to plan? When you're living on student loans and ramen noodles it may seem like making a budget is a frivolous exercise. But if you're living on your own you need to budget, whether you make $1,000 or $100,000 a year. Don't worry. A budget doesn't have to take days to create. And while it may sound restricting, it can actually be quite freeing. A good budget, combined with savvy spending, will help you survive your college years in good financial shape. This chapter will show you how by:

- teaching you how to create a budget that works
- outlining strategies for dealing with budget problems
- sharing tips for stretching your money

Create a Budget

A budget empowers you by giving you a true picture of your financial situation as well as a blueprint for making financial decisions. It's easy to think of things to want: a car, a vacation, graduate school. What's challenging is figuring out what actions you need to take now to be able to afford those things in the future.

Here's a simple approach to creating a budget that will work for you:

1. Calculate your income. How much money is coming in? Consider all sources, from scholarships, loans, grants, parents, jobs, investments, and savings.

2. Calculate your expenses. How much money is going out? This step takes a little more time because you don't want to leave anything out and there are probably all sorts of expenses to consider.

Monthly Expenses FIXED	
Rent/Room Cost	$800
Meal plan	$300
Utilities	$100
Insurance	$60
Tuition	$1000
Auto payment	$350
Credit card payment	$80
Total FIXED Expenses	**$2,690**

Monthly Expenses VARIABLE	
Entertainment	$100
Transportation	$50
Clothing	$100
Eating Out	$75
Personal Care (haircuts, etc.)	$150
Gifts	$50
Other	$50
Total VARIABLE Expenses	**$575**

Some expenses are **fixed**. In other words, they occur regularly and are usually in the same amount. Examples of fixed monthly expenses are things like rent, basic phone service, and car payments. Other fixed expenses occur quarterly or annually. Examples of these include tuition bills and auto insurance premiums.

Record your monthly fixed expenses. For annual or semi-annual expenses, record the cost per month (for example, if your auto insurance premium is $1,200 annually, write down $100 per month).

Other expenses are **variable**. This means that they vary from month to month and you have some control over how much you spend on them. For example, a person might spend $300 on food one month and $500 the next. One-time expenses are variable, as well.

So what amounts should you use for your variable expense categories? To construct a workable budget, you'll want to figure out your average monthly expenses. Keep a spending journal. Review your actual expenses from a two-month period and add up every purchase. If you use cash for most of your purchases, collect receipts or write down your expenses as you go through your day. For debit card purchases, you can use your bank statement to itemize your expenses.

Keep a Spending Journal

For 1 – 2 months, keep track of everything you spend. There are four common approaches to this mission. Try one or a combination of several:

Keep every receipt and itemize your spending at the end of each day

OR

Carry a small notebook with you where you can note each expense

OR

If you use your debit card for most purchases, review your account records online at the end of each week and itemize expenses then.

OR

If you use your debit card for most purchases, review your transactions and itemize them using budgeting software (e.g., Quicken) or an online budgeting website such as www.mint.com

3. Create an income statement.

Once you know your income and expenses, you can draft an income statement:

> **Monthly income**
> **— Expenses (fixed and variable)**
> _____
> **= Net income**

An income statement will help you see your monthly bottom line. If your average income minus your average expenses equals an average negative balance, you know you'll need to make some adjustments: make more money or spend less.

4. Make a plan.

After you've assessed your income and expenses as they are, you can make a plan for a financially sustainable lifestyle. Write down all of your fixed numbers—the income and expenses that can't or won't change in the near future. Then, take a second look at your variable expenses: Are there places you could nip and tuck that would leave your bank account looking better at the end of each month? Are there variable expenses that you haven't included that you need to plan for (example: gifts, spring break, or a bike tune up)?

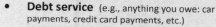

Common Expense Categories

- **Housing**
- **Utilities**
- **Debt service** (e.g., anything you owe: car payments, credit card payments, etc.)
- **Insurance** (e.g., auto, health, renter's insurance)
- **Transportation** (e.g., bus fare, gas)
- **Entertainment** (e.g., movies, eating out, etc.)
- **Personal** (e.g., food, clothing, health club fees)
- **Contributions and gifts**

People who don't budget spend erratically—splurging here, denying themselves there—and feel anxious all the time because they don't know what to expect when they open their bank statement or bills. When you budget you can make rational decisions based on your plan. You might still be broke, but at least you'll be able to evaluate the situation wisely. You might even decide to change your fixed expenses by, say, renting a cheaper place or selling your car.

Tips for Stretching Your Money

Here are some time-tested tips for surviving on a student budget:

Use coupons. If you're going to buy something, you might as well spend a little time to get the best deal. Apps like Coupons.com and Grocery Pal make it easy to find out about deals local businesses are offering.

Shop sales. Just about everything goes on sale eventually. When you see something you want, watch and wait for it to go on sale. You can also ask a salesperson when the item is likely to go on sale so that you'll know when to beeline it to the store. Some grocery stores have select times of the month for reduced prices. Once you know what those days are, you can plan your major grocery trips accordingly.

> Creating a budget is not a one-time event. Review, reevaluate, and revise your budget regularly.

Comparison shop. It takes more time, but when you want or need to make a purchase it's worth checking out your options. Look for store circulars, or use an app like Shop Savvy or Wishbone to find who is offering the best deal on the things you want.

Ask for a deal. Sometimes all you have to do is ask. Call your credit card company and ask for a lower interest rate or to have a fee waived. Ask a sales-clerk if you can get the sale price now or if you can at least hold the item until the sale.

Find freebies. College is full of freebies if you know where to look. You can snack on samples at local grocery stores, find promotional gifts, and attend company-sponsored free events.

Flash your student I.D. Many businesses offer discounts to students and some of them don't advertise that they do. Ask if you're not sure, and always carry your student I.D. with you just in case.

Spend to save. Sometimes you have to spend money to save money. For example, spending $30 every three months to change your car's oil is costly—but not as much as having to replace your car's engine when it runs out of oil.

Live simply. Reconsider all the things you "need" to have. Cable television, a gym membership, new books…you might surprise yourself with how well you adapt to life without these "necessities."

Wait before you buy. Impulse shopping can blast a good budget to shreds. Resolve to wait 48 hours before making a purchase of something you want but don't need. If, after 48 hours, you still feel you can't live without it, figure out how to pay for it and make the purchase. You'll find that you end up making purchases that you truly appreciate and don't regret.

Budgeting Made Easy **Exercises**

1. Keep a spending journal. For one week, write down every penny you spend and categorize each item you buy. Write a one-page reflection on what you learned about your spending habits.

2. Review your fixed expenses. Are there ways to reduce any of them? How would you go about reducing some of your fixed expenses? What would you sacrifice? What would you gain?

3. Review your variable expenses. Which categories cost you the most each month? How would you go about reducing some of your variable expenses? What would you sacrifice? What would you gain?

4. Research the best deals for college students in your community and present your findings to the class. You may choose to focus on a theme—for example, *Cheap Eats*, or *Entertainment*.

Visit **www.LifeDuringCommunityCollege.com**
for more resources and exercises.

Banking

CHAPTER 23

They come bearing gifts of free t-shirts and water bottles. Sometimes they even offer gift cards or cash. While your piggy bank sat mutely in the corner of your room, these banks send cheerful representatives to campus to sign you up for a new checking account. You need a bank, they need customers. It's a win, win situation, right?

Right. Except that banks are in the business of making money and you'll want to make sure the bank you choose doesn't make too much money off of you. Consider this: the average checking account costs over $150 annually, according to a 2014 MoneyRates.com report. Free checking is no exception, as the fees for ATM and teller use, automatic bill payment, check writing, and overdrafts mount up. We know one college student who was shocked when she added up all the fees she had paid over a one year period—and realized it was over $800!

Avoiding such financial disasters doesn't mean you have to keep your money tucked away in a box under your bed; you just need to choose—and use—your checking account wisely.

This chapter will:

- help you choose a bank that makes sense for you
- discuss how to open a bank account
- teach you how to keep track of your account balance
- offer you money-saving tips for using banking services

Choosing a Bank

You have three main choices: a bank with physical locations, an online bank, or a credit union. Banks and credit unions offer similar services, but differ in whom they serve and how they do business. Banks want to make a profit, and do so by charging service fees and offering low interest rates on deposits. Credit unions, on the other hand, are nonprofit and are owned by the members they serve. Their business model allows them to offer services at a much lower cost and to provide higher rates on deposits. However, credit unions are not open to everybody, they usually have a limited number of branches and a smaller network of ATMs, and they tend to offer a limited range of services. If you are eligible to join a credit union, it may be a good choice for you, but make sure you consider all potential costs before you make a decision.

Traditional banks with physical branches are the most common choice for students. There might even be bank branches on your college campus. Most traditional banks will offer a student checking account that has low to no monthly maintenance fees. They count on the fact that college students will rack up fees that offset the free checking. (Every bank has different fees, but some common ones to be aware of include fees for dipping below the minimum monthly balance, bouncing a check, or using a non-affiliated ATM.) Traditional banks generally have online banking services so you can do most of your banking from the comfort of your dorm room.

Online banks are another option. They usually offer free or low-cost checking accounts and services, and may have better interest rates than traditional banks. Some even offer no-fee ATM use at any ATM, which can be a bonus when you're out on the town or when you travel home for breaks. They have fees for overdrafts and non-sufficient funds and the like, of course. One downside of choosing an online bank is that it may be inconvenient to make deposits. You may have to set up automatic deposits or send the checks to them in the mail, though some banks offer convenient at-home deposit options where you can submit a deposit using your smartphone.

Evaluate your banking needs before you make a decision. Review your previous banking habits, as well as your current situation. Consider where you will live throughout the year and what kind of banking you think you will need. Be realistic about your banking habits and needs. (You've got enough to do just figuring out new classes and how to get along with a roommate.)

Your Banking Needs	
How many checks will I need to write a month?	
How many ATM withdrawals will I want to make per month?	
What kind of minimum monthly balance—if any—can I count on maintaining?	
What are my online banking needs and preferences?	
Do I ever overdraw my account?	
Do I want to earn interest on my deposits?	
Will my primary banking be done online or at the bank branch?	
Do I tend to keep track of my account balance?	
Will other people, such as my parents, be making deposits into the account? How can I make it easy for them to do so?	

Visit **www.LifeDuringCommunityCollege.com**
for more resources and exercises.

Once you figure out how you're likely to use a checking account, consider the options available to you. Here are some items you can evaluate in order to comparison shop:

- Interest rates
- Online banking features
- Number and location of ATMs
- ATM fees
- Deposit options
- Loan services
- Credit card/Debit card services
- Bill pay options

- Federal Deposit Insurance
- Fees and requirements
- Alerts and protection against fraud
- Money market accounts
- Convenience of locations
- Overdraft protection
- Brokerage services
- Reward points for credit card or debit card use

Before you sign up with a bank, find out how other people will be able to make deposits into your account and what kind of information those other people will need in order to do so. Many students will receive at least periodic monetary assistance from parents and other people, so it makes sense to choose a bank account that makes it easy for them to make deposits.

Opening a Bank Account

You may open a bank account in person, online, or by mail. If you are under eighteen, your parents or guardians will need to cosign to open the account. One good thing about such an account, called a joint account, is that your parents or guardians will be able to deposit money easily. They will also be able to review your spending and deposit records, which may be helpful or a drawback, depending on your perspective. A potential drawback from their perspective is that, as cosigners, they will be liable to cover your overdrafts or other banking problems. Some students start with a joint account and then, when they turn eighteen, they switch to an individual account.

Whether you are opening a joint or individual account, you will also probably need two pieces of identification and an address.

If you do open a joint account with your parents, have a conversation about expectations they (and you) have of how that joint account will be managed. Money can be a hot topic of conversation, and the last thing you and your parents need in this time of transition is tension about banking issues. Some parents, for instance, will want to maintain control over their first-year college student's spending and saving habits; others simply make deposits and do not pay much attention to their son or daughter's bank account details.

Keep Track of Your Account

If someone offered to pay you $200 to balance their accounts correctly, would you do it? When you balance your own account and avoid costly mistakes like overdrafts and additional fees, you get to keep more of your money. Here are some ways to manage your account without making it a full-time job:

- Keep track of debit card purchases and ATM transactions

- Use duplicate checks so you have copies for your reference

- Note when you make deposits and when the funds will be available

- Keep receipts for purchases, withdrawals, and deposits

- Establish a regular time each week to review your accounts and update any activities you may have forgotten

- Set up your online banking so you can check your account balances and recent activity

It's important to check your account balance regularly. Doing so will help you avoid any surprises that can crop up, such as an overdrawn account or a faulty deposit.

Tips to Help You Save

Know what part of "free" means "fee." Sure, your bank will charge fees for some services. If you know what they are you can avoid getting stuck paying for them.

Use direct deposit. Many banks will waive certain fees if you use direct deposit. If your employers offer direct deposit, sign up for it.

Maintain a minimum balance. Banks calculate your minimum balance in one of two ways: daily minimum balance, which requires you to maintain the balance every single day, and average daily balance, which requires you to maintain the balance as an average over the billing cycle. Make sure you choose a realistic balance option—if you have a choice between the two—and maintain the balance required by your bank.

Opt in for overdraft protection. Sometimes things happen that are beyond your control. For example, you might write a series of checks and then realize your student loan funds were never deposited. With overdraft protection, banks advance you the money to cover the checks you have written. There are usually fees for this service. Know what your bank's policy and procedures are and how much overdrafts might end up costing you.

Ask for discounts and waived fees. Once your bank has you as a customer, they want to keep you. Don't be shy about asking your bank for a better deal or to waive certain fees.

Be smart about using services:

- **Know where your bank's no-fee ATMs are located.** If you use ATMs that are not part of your bank's system, you will be charged an average of $2.77 per transaction, according to Bankrate.com's most recent survey of checking accounts. Often, you will be charged twice: once by your bank and again by the ATM company.

- **Request cash when you use your debit card to make purchases.** Most banks don't charge fees for "cash back" transactions.

- **Limit transactions and bank visits** if your checking account has a maximum number of such services allowed per month. However, it's important to note that there are so many banking options available that you shouldn't have to settle for a bank that limits transactions and bank visits.

- **Don't order checks from your bank.** Most banks charge between $12 and $17 for a box of 250 checks. A cheaper option is to order checks directly from the check-printing company. Find these companies online.

- **Use online bill pay options.** You'll save on stamps and checks. Also, you can set up automatic payments so you won't get stuck paying the fees vendors charge for late payments.

Banking Exercises

1. Fill out the chart on page 163, then compare three specific banking options available to you. Which option do you think will be the best fit for your banking needs and habits?

2. Research online money tracking sites that can help you manage your account. Some of them categorize expenses, send alerts when funds are low, and help you visualize your cash flow with charts and graphs. Your bank probably offers such online services. If they don't, research online or check out money tracking apps like Mint, Spendee, and BUDGT.

3. Make a banking action plan and post it where you'll remember to follow it. Your action plan might include a schedule for bill paying and balancing your checking account, a method for keeping track of receipts and transactions, and ways to leverage your bank use (for instance, can you pay for your tuition with a debit card that earns you airline miles?).

Visit **www.LifeDuringCommunityCollege.com**
for more resources and exercises.

Your Credit

CHAPTER 24

Somewhere, even as you read this, your life is being summarized as a series of entries about what you owe, what you buy, and how timely you pay your bills. Every time you do something to affect your credit—sign up for a new credit card, make a late payment, complete a loan application—it is recorded in a report that may be read by future lenders, landlords, and even employers.

Why is everyone so interested in your credit report? What does it reveal about you? Think of it as a credit report card that provides a snapshot of your financial responsibility. It's a record of every time you apply for or accept a loan or other form of credit. It also tracks how you use your credit—how much you have available, how much you owe, and how you repay. The people who will be considering granting you a student loan or giving you a new credit card want to know your financial track record.

Do you know what your credit report contains? If not, you should. Even if you haven't used credit much at this point in your life, you need to be watchful to make sure someone else isn't using it for you.

This chapter will tell you what you need to know about credit. We will:

- explain what a credit report is
- outline the importance of credit reports
- tell you how to obtain a free copy of your credit report
- describe how to maintain good credit

What is a Credit Report?

A credit report is a detailed history of your borrowing habits for the past seven to ten years. Your credit report is a record of what you owe and to whom, what you've paid, and if you've made any late payments. It also reveals personal information, such as your social security number, current and former addresses and telephone numbers. Any time you order a report or authorize someone else to do so, the inquiry is recorded. Several companies called credit bureaus compile and maintain databases for the purpose of creating such reports.

According to federal law, credit bureaus are allowed to give your credit report to the following parties:

- Creditors who are considering giving you credit

- Employers considering you for employment, promotion, reassignment, or retention

- Insurers considering you for an insurance policy or reviewing an existing policy

- Government agencies reviewing your financial status or government benefits

- Anyone with a legitimate business need for the information, such as a potential landlord

- Parties who have a court order or federal jury subpoena for your credit report

- A third party to whom you have requested, in writing, that your credit report be issued

There are two kinds of inquiries made regarding your credit. **"Hard" inquiries** are when you seek to obtain credit or when you authorize someone access to your full credit report. **"Soft" inquiries** are requests for general information rather than a full credit history. Examples of soft inquiries include when you request a copy of your own credit report and when a company is gathering marketing information about potential customers.

Credit Report vs. Credit Score

Credit Report: A detailed record of what you owe and to whom, what you've paid, if you've made any late payments, and where you've lived.

Credit Score: A shorthand way for a lender to tell if you're a good credit risk or not. A high score means you're a lower risk and have a better chance of obtaining credit at better interest rates. While each credit bureau has its own system, they all take into account the following factors: your ability to make payments on time, the amount of credit you owe, the type of credit you owe, the length of your credit history (the longer the better), and the number of requests for new credit.

Why is My Credit Important?

Your credit report and credit score might seem irrelevant at this point in your life, but they are very important. Good credit opens doors and lowers rates. Here are just a few things credit can affect:

Insurance rates. Many insurance companies use credit scores to decide whether to offer a customer car insurance and how much to charge him or her for it.

Your ability to secure a loan. If your credit score indicates you are a credit risk, you may be denied credit.

Interest rates on loans and credit. People with a good credit history get better interest rates and more credit made available to them. For example, someone with an excellent FICO credit score (720 – 850) might be able to secure a 36 month auto loan at an interest rate of 4.953%. Someone with a fair FICO score (660 – 689) would qualify for an auto loan at a much higher interest rate, say 8.347%. (FICO stands for Fair Isaac Corporation, one of the major credit score reporting agencies.) The difference in monthly payments on a $10,000 car would be $16, or over $570 over the life of the loan. On larger loans the difference is even more significant, of course. Someone with an excellent credit score might pay as much as $4,800 less on a $100,000 30-year fixed mortgage than someone with merely a good credit score. (Check out **www.myfico.com** for credit score/loan amount calculators.)

Employment. Some employers use credit history to assess a job applicant's responsibility and reliability. If an employer or potential employer denies you employment, a promotion, or security clearance because of your credit history, they are required by law to let you know and to give you time to review your report and respond.

Your ability to rent an apartment. Landlords want to know if their potential tenants are likely to pay rent on time. People with better credit scores may be more likely to secure a rental unit—and less likely to pay a huge deposit.

Get Your Free Credit Report

The Fair Credit Reporting Act requires each of the nationwide consumer reporting companies (Equifax, Experian, and TransUnion) to provide you with a free copy of your credit report, at your request, once every 12 months. You need to be proactive with your credit. Check it now and address any problems immediately.

Conventional wisdom says it takes years to remove a blemish from a credit report, but seconds to put one on. Checking your credit report on a regular basis will enable you to monitor and prevent any illegal use of your credit.

Get Your Free Credit Report Now!

www.annualcreditreport.com
877-322-8228

The three major credit bureaus (Equifax, Experian, and TransUnion) are required by federal law to give consumers one FREE credit report each year. When you go to their websites you might find other services for sale. Don't worry about that stuff yet. Just get the free report.

Ordering a credit report DOES NOT affect your credit score. Applying for a credit card DOES affect your credit score.

Avoiding credit cards might make good financial sense, but it doesn't help you build credit. The best thing to do at this point in your financial life is to obtain credit, use it, and pay it off. That way you'll have a solid history for future lenders to review—and you'll be more likely to get the mortgage or business loan you want in the future.

Even responsible people can end up with dings on their credit report. Here's how to keep your report nice and shiny:

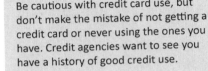

Build good credit:

1) Get credit
2) Use it
3) Pay it off

Be cautious with credit card use, but don't make the mistake of not getting a credit card or never using the ones you have. Credit agencies want to see you have a history of good credit use.

Know what you owe, know who you owe, and pay your bills on time.

When you move, make sure every business you deal with has your change of address on file. You don't want to miss a payment because the vendor is sending bills to an old residence!

Set up a folder in your email account for e-bills, as they can easily get buried in the inbox.

Don't miss a payment. Remember: Inadvertently missing a payment—even missing one payment because of the vendor's mistake—can cause as much headache as blatantly ignoring a due date.

Repairing your credit is another challenge, but it's a process worth starting now if your credit report is less than stellar. Here are some ways to repair your credit effective immediately:

Need help repairing your credit? Your first stop should be the Federal Trade Commission website at **www.ftc.gov.** Beware of credit repair scams!

Set up a system today for paying all current bills on time.

If you have big outstanding balances that you can't pay off, contact the business to see if they'll negotiate a payment plan with you. Vendors lose a lot of money when they send accounts to collections agencies, so they'll probably be willing to work with you.

Vendors recoup pennies on the dollar when they send accounts to collections. They usually prefer to work with customers and arrange a payment plan rather than go through collections.

If you see an error on your credit report, document it right away. Write a letter to the credit bureau explaining your dispute, send in any information that substantiates your claim, and request that the error be corrected. Inform the creditor as well. Remember to make copies of all related paperwork and keep careful records.

Your Credit **Exercises**

1. You probably saw this one coming: Check your credit report now. Go to **www.annualcreditreport.com** and request a free credit report. Review it. If there are any errors, address them as soon as possible.

2. At this point in your life, do you need to build, maintain, or repair your credit? Decide on two action steps you can do this week to improve your credit. Tell a partner what your actions steps are, then report back to him or her when you've completed them.

3. If you were an employer, would you want to know the credit histories of your prospective employees? Explain. Do you think it is right for an employer to have access to this information?

4. Debt accumulation among college students is at an all-time high. Do you think policies or required programs should be put into place to correct this situation? If so, why? If not, what do you think would help improve the situation?

Visit **www.LifeDuringCommunityCollege.com**
for more resources and exercises.

Credit Card and Debt Management

CHAPTER 25

The Freshman 15 is nothing. Let's talk about the college graduate 30,000. We're not talking pounds here, of course, but dollars in debt. Debt is money owed to a creditor. According to Sallie Mae and the U.S. Department of Education National Center for Education Statistics, the average undergraduate college student graduates with over $29,400 in student loan debt and over $3,000 in credit card debt. Yikes!

The college years are not just about personal growth, it turns out. They're also about credit, debt, and other financial management topics. And you'll want to get financially savvy now or you could end up graduating with a diploma and a mountain of debt.

You do not have to join the ranks of students who are inordinately burdened by debt. While your circumstances may require you to accumulate some debt during your college years, you can do so wisely. This chapter will show you how by:

- helping you understand debt
- recommending strategies to keep your debt in check
- teaching you how to recognize if your debt is out of control
- outlining your options if your debt becomes overwhelming

Understanding Debt

If you have debt, you are not alone in your age group. Recent statistics illustrate the reality of undergraduate student loan and credit card debt:

- In 2012, 70% of college students graduated with student loan debt. **(source: projectsonstudentdebt.org)**
- From 2008 to 2012, average student loan debt increased 6% per year. **(source: projectsonstudentdebt.org)**
- 1 in 10 students graduate with over $40,000 in student loans. **(source: projectsonstudentdebt.org)**
- Undergraduate students' average monthly credit card balance is over $3,000. **(source: Sallie Mae)**
- Almost 7% of debtors applying for bankruptcy are between the ages of 18 and 24. **(source: Government Accountability Office)**

While these figures may seem alarming, it's important to recognize that not all debt is bad.

Good Debt vs. Bad Debt

Good debt is debt that allows you to access something of long-term value, such as an education or a home. Bad debt is the result of short-term, "feel-good" decisions, such as purchasing something you can't really afford and don't really need. Student loans that help further your education will probably pay off in nonmaterial as well as material ways. Statistically, people with post-secondary degrees do much better in the job market than those who don't have them. Because of the importance of a college education, student loans are generally viewed as low-interest, high return investments. Much like home loans, they promise higher future income. Also, both of these types of debts offer tax advantages—you can write off a portion of the interest, which pulls down the cost of the debt itself. In certain situations, you may qualify for loan forgiveness and cancellation programs.

55% of students who took out loans for their education feel burdened by their debt.

54% of student borrowers said they'd take out less in loans if they had to do it all over again.

70% of student borrowers said student loans were worth incurring for personal growth.

Source: Nellie Mae 2002 National Student Loan Survey.

Visit this website to find out more: **https://studentaid.ed.gov/sa/repay-loans/forgiveness-cancellation**

Credit card debt can be in both categories. It's good in that accumulating some debt and paying it off is necessary for establishing good credit. It's also good because it's convenient and secure. You're not likely to rush to the airlines to pay for a flight with a wad of cash; you're even less likely to call the bank to put a stop payment on the cash someone lifted from your wallet. Credit cards allow you to book flights and hotels, they provide extra insurance for some purchases, and they tend to be much better than cash when you travel and want to get the best exchange rate. Credit cards can be stolen, but they're usually protected. This means you probably won't be responsible for charges racked up illegally with your card.

But the praise stops there. Credit card debt can be very bad. Interest rates that begin as low, introductory rates quickly become unmanageably high. When you can't pay more than the minimum monthly payment, you end up paying doubly and even triply for that cool gear you bought five years ago. How bad is credit card debt? It depends on how much you owe. How long will it take you to pay the debt down? How high is the interest rate? Is it limiting other opportunities, like your ability to apply for another type of loan? The answers to these questions will tell you if your credit card load has moved from bad to ugly.

Let's say you charge $2,000 on a credit card to cover part of your tuition one semester. If that credit card company charges 19% interest and you make the minimum monthly payments, it will take you over 8 years and almost another $2,000 in interest to pay off that charge.

Source: Government Accountability Office.

Keeping Debt in Check

In the whirl of classes, financial aid paperwork, and new freedoms, many students quickly lose track of what they owe and to whom. Be aware of for-profit companies that prey on people who feel overwhelmed by debt. You should not have to pay anyone to manage your debt situation; there's plenty you can do on your own and if you feel really buried there are well-respected nonprofit organizations, like National Foundation for Credit Counseling, that can help you. Here's how to get a handle on your debt:

Step 1: Figure out what you owe. Pull out your latest credit card and student loan statements and create a table of the following: the amount you owe to each vendor, the interest rates, and your minimum monthly payments. (Note: Go to www.nslds.ed.gov, the National Student Loan Data System website, to see all of your student loans in one handy place.) Your student loan payments won't begin until you graduate, but it's good to keep track of them starting now. It is also important to know that student loan debt cannot be forgiven due to bankruptcy.

Debt Record					
Name of loan	Principal owed	Interest rate	Annual interest payment (est.)	Minimum monthly payment	Goal monthly payment
BankTwo Visa	$5,522	15.75%	$5,522 X 0.1575 = $870	$65	$150
Fuel Card	$648	11.25%	$648 X 0.1125 = $73	$20	$80

Step 2: Prioritize pay offs. You need to make the minimum monthly payments on all debts or your credit score will suffer. But creditors' required minimum monthly payments are designed to pad their pockets and raid yours, so do all you can to pay more than the minimum. Pay off higher interest loans first. If Card A has an 18% interest rate and Card B has a 9% interest rate, pay the minimum on B and pay off A as quickly as possible.

Step 3: Consolidate debt. You don't need to do this "officially," using a for-profit company to manage your accounts. You can usually take care of this step on your own. For example, pull all your credit card debt onto one low-interest card. It will lower your overall interest payments and allow you to pay one bill instead of several, thereby increasing the odds of paying the bill on time and keeping your credit score up. Caution: Do not use your new card to charge items or you'll likely end up with more debt than when you started the transfer process.

Step 4: Live within your means. Stop all impulse buying and cut corners where you can. Pack food with you to class so you won't be tempted by the campus eateries. When a new gadget or item catches your eye, give yourself a cool-off period of at least 48 hours to consider the pros and cons of purchasing it. It can be empowering to say no to such purchases, especially when you realize how doing so will benefit your future.

Step 5: Stay focused. Keep your debt and your financial priorities in view. Review your statements and always be able to answer those fundamental questions: How much do I owe? Can I handle that much debt? The students who end up buried by debt are usually shocked when they realize how much they've racked up. Don't let unnecessary debt sneak up on you.

Debt Record					
Name of loan	Principal owed	Interest rate	Annual interest payment (est.)	Minimum monthly payment	Goal monthly payment

Is Your Debt Out of Control?

If any of these statements describe you, your debt has moved into the driver's seat:

_____ I shop impulsively, buying things I don't really need.

_____ I make late or minimum monthly payments.

_____ I have credit cards that are at, or close to, my credit limit.

_____ I'm not sure how much I really owe.

_____ I use cash advances to pay my bills.

_____ I've had my credit card declined.

_____ My family or friends are concerned about my spending habits.

If you recognize yourself in these statements, you can take action now to take back control.

Here are a couple of options:

Contact a counselor at the National Foundation for Credit Counseling (www.nfcc.org), a nonprofit organization that offers education and credit counseling. There are plenty of unethical credit counseling services, so make sure you stick to vetted, respected ones.

Contact your creditors. Call your current credit card companies and ask them to lower the interest rates. Creditors often want to work with their customers. After all, they want their money. If you can't pay them they'll end up having to send your account to collections, which means a big loss for them.

If one or more of your creditors has turned your account over to a collection agency, you need to know the following:

- A collection agency may contact you by phone, email, mail, or in person.

- They cannot call your boss or members of your family.

- No one else can be forced to pay a debt that is yours alone.

- You can get them to stop calling you by sending them a letter. They are then only allowed to contact you regarding plans to bring legal action against you.

- You do not need to tolerate rude or belittling remarks.

- Collection agencies are not empowered to work out terms of payment.

- If you think you are being treated unfairly, contact the FTC at (877) FTC-HELP or go to **www.ftc.gov**.

If you don't make your loan payments, you risk going into default. Defaulting on your loan has serious consequences. Your school, the financial institution that made or owns your loan, your loan guarantor, and the federal government all can take action to recover the money you owe. Understand how missing a loan payment can be a problem, what default means and the consequences of default, and what you need to do if your loan is in default or if you think the default on your loan is an error. (Student Aid. ed.gov/sa/repay-loans/default)

Credit Cards & Debt Management **Exercises**

1. Fill out the table ("Debt Record") on page 175. How long will it take you to pay off your current bad debt? The National Foundation for Credit Counseling website (**www.nfcc.org**) has a great calculator that can help you answer this question.

2. Go to **www.consumer.ftc.gov** and review the sections on choosing a credit counseling organization, and debt management plans.

3. Develop a plan for keeping your debt load as low as possible. How can you limit spending now so that you're not paying for it well into the future? Remember to keep your goals in plain sight—literally, write them where you can see them on a regular basis.

Visit **www.LifeDuringCommunityCollege.com**
for more resources and exercises.

Your Career

CHAPTER 26

Prepare now for the career of your future, whether that career begins next week or in a few years. In some ways, your transition from community college to the workplace will be smooth. After all, you've likely learned the current best practices in your profession and have been trained in the latest technologies. Also, college students, like most professionals, often work under deadline and sometimes with a team of people. Have confidence that your education and training has prepared you well. This chapter is about what you can do now to get your career off to a great start.

Ten Steps to Career Success

1. Get to the Career Center NOW

We recommend that students begin visiting their campus Career Center early in their first year of college. It is an invaluable resource: you'll find a helpful staff and everything you need to map out your major and career plans. It's also the go-to place to find out about internships, events, workshops, career fairs, and employer information sessions. Many career centers also provide mock interviews along with guidance on how to write an effective resumé.

2. Make connections

You've heard the saying "It's all about who you know." However, a more accurate statement is "It's all about who knows you." Developing a group of contacts and mentors—in other words, networking—is one of the most important things you can do in your early career.

Networking keeps you tapped in to the ideas, trends, and information that are relevant to your profession, makes you more visible, and helps you connect with others. However, networking doesn't necessarily come naturally. Like any other skill, it must be developed.

So, how do you build your network? First, determine who you already know, from family and friends to advisors and supervisors. Second, consider additional avenues for networking, including professional groups, educational opportunities, and volunteer work. Third, maintain a professional online presence, especially on dedicated networking websites such as LinkedIn as well as in online groups related to your profession.

Do: Stay in contact, be sincere, and be respectful. Ask permission before sharing anybody's contact information. If someone does something nice for you, thank them. Also, be helpful. Think about what you have to offer, whether that's information, contacts, skills, or support.

Don't: Call excessively, link to someone who doesn't know you, or come across as if you are always looking for a favor.

Ultimately, networking is all about relationships. And the best relationships are mutually enriching. Consider your role in your network: there will be times when you'll need to call on others for assistance, advice, and favors and other times when you'll be the one assisting, advising, and doing what you can to help somebody else out.

3. Consider an internship

Internships are the best way to break into many careers, and many graduates spend time interning before they're hired in their field. Sometimes colleges coordinate internships for students or graduates. Other times, you'll hear about internships from your contacts or by checking postings on sites like **www.internships.com** or on organizations' websites. Or you might even create your own internship opportunity: if you're really interested in a particular organization, consider approaching them with an internship proposal. Even if they say no, you'll have demonstrated initiative and made a positive impression.

Your time is at a premium and the last thing you want to do is to commit to something that doesn't help you develop skills and experience. Sure, you can expect some drudgery in an internship, but it should also help you expand your understanding of your profession. Make sure that you fully understand the job description and expectations, and determine if the position will help you hone your skills and experience. If possible, find out what other students or graduates have experienced when working for the company or organization. Finally, take into account what kind of compensation you'll receive—whether that's financial or academic credit—as well as expenses you might incur (transportation, wardrobe, etc.) if you accept the position.

4. Prepare for and practice interviewing

Whether you're aiming for full time employment or an internship, you'll want to master the art of the interview. As we mentioned at the beginning of this chapter, the Career Center and its website will likely be one of your best resources when it comes to interviewing. Many career centers host opportunities for mock interviews or offer access to online practice interview programs. Of course, an online search will also turn up a wealth of information about interviewing.

A successful job candidate:

- **Prepares for a variety of questions.** There are standard interview questions ("Why do you want this job?") and off-the-wall interview questions ("How would you teach someone else how to make a sandwich?"). Familiarize yourself with the typical questions and consider how you'd answer each one succinctly and positively. Have some fun online looking through more wildcard interview questions and imagining what you'd say in response. The more exposure and experience you have, the more flexible and relaxed you'll be when you get to the real thing.

- **Does his or her homework.** Read through the company or organization's website. Consider its mission statement, values, and culture. Think about what you can offer the organization and how you might fit into it.

- **Practices listening.** Sure, your interview answers are important, but listening attentively is also necessary. When you listen well, you convey interest and engagement, qualities all employers value. The best part about practicing this skill is you can do it almost anywhere anytime.

- **Has a strategy.** Think through what aspects of your personality and experience you most want to "sell" in the interview and how you'll go about doing that. You might even prepare some "soundbites" that you'll have at the ready. For example, if you've had training in a particular area that you think is relevant to the organization and they don't directly ask about it, you could find a way to plug it into your response to a question that they do ask.

- **Rehearses.** You'll want as much experience as possible with hypothetical interview situations before you interview for a position that you really want. Take advantage of your school's resources, as well as any friends or family who are willing to help you practice. If video or audio recording is an option for these mock interviews, do it. It's often difficult to watch or listen to ourselves, but it's so important to know how we come across to others. If you notice you have a fidgeting habit that is painfully apparent when you review tape of your mock interview, great! Better to see it now so that you can correct it when it's time for the real thing.

5. Polish your resumé

Your resumé will be a work in progress throughout your career. After all, you'll be revising it as you develop your skills and experience. At this stage, your goal is to craft a resumé that gets you in the door. What that looks like and the kind of information it contains depends upon you, your field, and the organizations you're interested in. A graphic designer's resumé and a nurse's resumé will look quite different.

You'll find all sorts of valuable resumé advice and templates online, and can choose the style and tips that match your career goals. What everybody needs, no matter what their profession, is reviewers, and the more the better. Ask the staff at the career center, a mentor or trusted advisor, and anyone else who would be willing to provide objective feedback to review your resumé.

6. Make a good first impression

Your first days and weeks on the job will make an impression on your new colleagues and supervisors. Here's how to make it a good one:

- **Project a positive attitude.** Positive, energetic, curious, eager to work— all of these are traits of successful people. On the days when you feel low energy or overwhelmed, making a conscious choice to focus on the positive will help you feel more balanced and may actually give you the energy you need.

- **Be professional.** Focus on work when you're at work. Make sure your verbal, nonverbal, and written communication reflects your professionalism. Dress appropriately for your work environment. For some organizations, that will be suits and for others that will mean wearing artfully frayed sweaters.

- **Respect your coworkers' time and expertise.** You'll probably need a lot of help figuring out organization procedures and protocols. Asking for guidance is a good way to get to know the people you work with—and, of course, necessary for doing a good job. If you need more than a few minutes of someone's time, ask if you can set up an appointment. That way he or she will know that you value his or her expertise and time.

- **Connect with all players.** Everyone in the organization is important. Cultivate a positive working relationship with people in your department and other departments, as well as with support staff.

7. Understand the organization

Each organization has a unique personality, made up of its values, structures, and norms. Because job satisfaction directly relates to how well the organization's personality meshes with your own, you'll want to decode the culture as soon as possible. Take into account the organization's

- **Mission and vision.** Is there a clear, shared mission? Do your coworkers speak positively about the organization and its leadership?

- **Expectations and support.** Are standards and expectations clearly defined and attainable? Do supervisors encourage and nurture employees' success on the job by giving timely and constructive feedback? Is there a clear evaluation/annual review system?

- **Physical office structure.** Does the office space, if there is one, promote collaboration or hierarchy, or something in between?

- **Work habits and hours.** What are the standard hours employees keep? What are productivity expectations? Is working from home encouraged and supported? Are employees expected to volunteer for additional projects?

- **Communication.** What are the common modes of communication used within the office? When there is tension, do the people involved treat each other respectfully?

- **Flexibility.** Does the organization allow or even encourage flexible work hours? Can employees job share or reduce their full time status if they choose to?

- **Resources.** Resources include technology, postage, food, and office supplies. How does one go about procuring office supplies? What kind of documentation is necessary?

- **Turnover.** Do people tend to stick around or does the organization have a more fluid workforce? Of the longstanding employees, who are the leaders and why?

Your organization's culture will have a profound effect on your life at work and outside of it. Keep your personal values and long-term professional goals in mind. If you're lucky, you'll have a good match, a place where you can comfortably learn and grow. However, even an imperfect match can be instructive.

8. Have realistic expectations

The most common complaint of new hires after two weeks on the job is that it wasn't what they expected. The good news is that's no longer a complaint after two months on the job. The lesson here is clear: Give it time. In the meantime, learn about the most frequent causes of new job dissatisfaction:

- **Dull, repetitive work.** It's natural to want to hit the ground running and prove yourself, but on the early days on the job new employees often find they're doing what feels like meaningless work. If that's the case for you, remember that it is typical to take on a support role when you first start a job. Everyone starts somewhere and when you prove that you're a team player you'll get more and more meaningful projects.

- **Conflict between what the organization needs and what the new employee needs.** The new employee wants challenging tasks; the supervisor needs to know the new employee is up for those tasks. The new employee wants autonomy; the supervisor needs evidence that the new employee is trustworthy.

New Employee Needs	Organization Needs (supervisor and coworkers)
Challenging tasks	To know that the new employee is competent
Autonomy	Evidence that new employee is trustworthy and understands his/her function in the organization
To feel valued	Proven commitment and loyalty
To feel he/she belongs and is liked	Evidence new employee is making an effort to fit in and respects others' time and space

- **Salary.** Many people just entering the workforce overestimate their initial salary potential as well as the frequency and rate of promotions. Raises, too, are on average much lower than people expect. The human resources department is a good place to start asking about standard salary practices for the organization. You can also look online for regional norms if you want to get a broader perspective.

- **Bosses.** Your direct supervisor will have a significant impact on your experience with the organization. Some bosses will be very hands on and helpful, some will be micromanagers, some will be hands off and hard to track down. Expect that it will take time to learn your boss's management and communication style.

- **Colleagues.** It's also typical to feel you don't fit in at first. Your new colleagues are busy and might not necessarily go out of their way to meet or collaborate with the new person. But take heart. With time you'll get to know each other and the relationships will develop naturally.

9. Communication in the workplace

As we mentioned before, each organization will have its own norms for communication. Here are some tips for effective professional communication, whether you're using email or IM:

- **Make your purpose clear.** If you're sending an email with a request, make that request plain. If you're leaving a voicemail, make it clear what you're asking or telling the recipient.

- **Use a professional tone and style.** Use correct spelling, punctuation, and forms of address. Make sure you'd feel comfortable if absolutely anybody in the organization read your message, even if you're just sending it to one person.

- **Be direct yet cordial.** Most working relationships depend on quick, informative, relatively informal communications. Be respectful of people's time by keeping things brief. Be mindful of tone by including cordial elements. A "Thank you!" means something different than a "Sincerely," which means something different from not signing off at all.

- **Give emails useful subject lines.** Your reader needs to know what the email is about before he or she even opens it.

- **CC with care.** When cc-ing someone, let the main recipient(s) as well as the cc'd person know why you've cc'd them.

- **When speaking on the phone, avoid multitasking**, such as keyboarding, texting, or—especially—eating.

- **Use IM sparingly** and only when you're sure it works for the other person. Some people don't like the interruptive nature of IM, so make sure you know if and when IM-ing is welcome.

10. Go beyond average

Going beyond expectations is what separates the above average professional from the remarkable one. Here's how to build a habit of excellence, which will not only impress your employers but give you job satisfaction:

- **Work a full day.** From the beginning days of your new job make sure that you're not only putting in the hours but that you're fully present during those hours. If you checkerboard your day with off-task moments, that line between work and home will get very blurry, which probably won't be good for your work life or your home life.

- **Do your job well.** Whatever your task, take pride in your work. See where it fits into the big picture—of your organization's needs as well as your professional goals.

- **Take initiative.** If you see a need in the organization and have insight into how to fill it, speak up. Examples we've seen: someone who volunteered to rewrite a computer program for his engineering firm, someone who created a style manual for her organization, and others who have offered to train colleagues in new technologies. Even taking on a small task, such as running copies, will demonstrate your willingness to work hard for the team.

- **Make the most of your mistakes.** Superior job performance includes dealing with mistakes in a constructive way. The below average employee covers up or blows off mistakes; the average employee minimizes his or her mistakes or transfers the blame; the excellent employee takes responsibility for the mistake, learns from it, and moves on. It's not a question if you'll make mistakes, but how you'll deal with them when you do.

- **Contribute positively to the organization.** Get in the habit of asking yourself if you are adding to the organization. The basic questions to ask yourself on a regular basis are, "What are my intentions?" and "What am I contributing?" Successful people communicate in a positive, intentional way. This doesn't mean being a yes man or yes woman. In fact, contributing positively sometimes means questioning the status quo or a colleague's ideas. But if your intentions are good and your methods respectful, you'll know you're adding something meaningful.

- **Join a professional association.** Joining a professional association will help you make connections and stay abreast of what's current in your field.

- **Continue your education.** Keep learning, get involved, and meet people who inspire you. You might take a class now that directly applies to your current job, but that leads to another, even more interesting job.

- **Volunteer and lead.** Volunteer work can have a meaningful, positive, and lasting impact on communities, families, and individuals. It's also good for your career. Volunteering provides

  - the opportunity to learn new skills, gain knowledge, and experiment with different interests,

  - exposure to different perspectives and experiences, and

  - a chance to establish contacts, build relationships, and foster mentors.

If you're lucky, you're surrounded by supervisors and colleagues who share a desire to be excellent. Such work environments can be incredible supportive of both the individual's and the company's needs, inspiring every employee to work beyond his or her potential. Whatever your actual job circumstances, set high expectations for your own performance and you'll feel more satisfaction and have more future opportunities.

It's an exciting place to be: on the cusp of a new career. There will be surprises and challenges, but you've got a solid background with your education and dedicated support from your college (especially, at this point in your life, the Career Center). That combined with your own initiative, hard work, and creativity will make the transition from college to the workplace a successful one. To maximize all the opportunities in your new career, be sure to read *Backpack to Briefcase, Steps to a Successful Career*. It's full of information and tips on excelling in your new career, including asking for your first raise!

Kickstart Your Career by Visiting:
www.CollegeTransitionPublishing.com

Planning for Continuing Education

CHAPTER 27

Depending on your career goal, transfer to a four-year college may or may not be a part of your immediate plan after graduation. For some community college graduates, immediate transfer to a four-year college is a given. This is especially true for those students earning an Associate of Arts degree, which is designed to be the transfer equivalent of the first two years of a bachelor's degree. For others, transfer to a four-year college may be an option pursued later on, after graduating from an Associate of Applied Science program, spending some time in the workforce, and finding that moving up the career ladder sometimes requires additional education. In either case, you will benefit from being familiar with the information and next steps outlined in this chapter as you plan for your transition to a four-year college.

Ten Steps to Successfully Transition to a Four-Year College

1. Start planning right away

By selecting your four-year transfer college early on, you can more efficiently plan for your bachelor's degree, and select courses that will satisfy requirements at both the community college and the four-year college. Having the correct information early on will help to avoid the disappointment of finding out that half of the courses you completed at the community college don't count toward the requirements of your bachelor's degree. Pinpointing the exact college you'll transfer to early in your community college experience can be a challenge. So, the best move is to select two or three colleges that offer your intended major and fit with your specific needs. Doing so will allow you to research the admission and degree requirements for each school, and make the proper connections with transfer advisors who can help determine which courses will be applied toward your bachelor's degree and any additional requirements you will need to satisfy prior to transfer.

2. Align your plan with your career goals

Is a bachelor's degree a necessary component of your career plan? Having a solid handle on your occupational choice and career goals will help you to determine the most commonly required credentials in your chosen field.

Visit **www.mynextmove.org** to research the necessary training and degree requirements, appropriate academic major, and to locate colleges offering the required credentials for your chosen career field.

3. Understand the benefits of completing the associate degree prior to transfer

Your chances of future success are greater if you complete your associate degree prior to transferring on to the four-year college. In one study, the bachelor degree completion rate was 72% for students who transferred after earning an associate degree, and only 56% for students who transferred without earning an associate degree (National Student Clearinghouse).

Unfortunately, most students are unaware of this statistic, and for various reasons choose to transfer prior to completing the associate degree. Put the odds of completing a baccalaureate degree in your favor by locking in that degree before moving on to the four-year college. Some four-year colleges will accept all associate degree credits toward the baccalaureate degree if the degree has been awarded prior to transfer. Another potential benefit is gaining junior standing, which offers the student additional privileges or waiver of certain requirements. Special scholarships may also be offered to associate degree holders. It's also great to have on your resumé and opens up employment opportunities while working on the baccalaureate degree.

Reverse transfer of credit as a back-up option. If circumstances are such that you must transfer prior to having earned the associate degree, check out your options to be awarded a reverse transfer (RT) associate degree. If you're only a few courses short of earning the associate degree at your community college, inquire about the option to complete those courses at the four-year college and transfer the credits back to your community college to satisfy the associate degree requirements.

4. Good grades now can pay off during transfer

Working hard in class and earning excellent grades is important for any student. However, it is particularly important when considering the financial benefits of transfer scholarships at four-year colleges. Top performing students can count on generous scholarships and excellent transfer packages at most four-year colleges. Here are a few examples:

Phi Theta Kappa (PTK) Scholarship. PTK is the official honor society for community colleges and offers over $90 million scholarships to eligible members. Four-year colleges recognize and actively recruit Phi Theta Kappa members for transfer, knowing they will be high performing students who are likely to successfully complete baccalaureate degrees at their institutions. Find out more at: **www.ptk.org**

Jack Kent Cooke Foundation Scholarship. This is the largest privately funded scholarship for transfer students. Individual awards are as high as $40,000 per year, and are awarded to up to 85 applicants each year. Scholarships are awarded to applicants with high academic achievement who also demonstrate leadership and meet financial-need criteria. Find out more at **www.jkcf.org**

Institution specific transfer scholarships. Most four-year colleges designate scholarships for transfer students. These scholarships can be competitive or may be automatically awarded based on criteria established by the four-year college. Visit with your transfer advisor to find out if there are specific scholarships you might qualify for, and begin working toward meeting the criteria early in your community college career.

5. Research your options

Once you've narrowed down your focus to two to three transfer colleges, you'll be able to more accurately research your options. In order to make an informed decision you'll want to do the following:

Attend transfer fairs. Most community colleges host transfer fair events that bring in transfer representatives from various public and private four-year colleges who are seeking to recruit community college graduates. This is a prime opportunity to make connections with transfer advisors, gather brochures, and ask important questions about the transfer requirements, processes, and scholarships for each transfer school. Collect business cards from transfer representatives, and follow up with them later as questions arise.

Visit four-year colleges. There's no better way to determine if a transfer school is the right fit for you. Touring the campus, meeting with program faculty, and exploring campus resources will help you weigh your options. Chances are you'll get a feel for which school is the best fit for you after you've taken time to visit and experience it for yourself.

Determine your needs. Do you need to stick close to home, or are you able to relocate? Do you prefer an on-campus learning environment, or is a distance learning program a better fit? Are there particular extra-curricular interests that you'd like to pursue? Can they offer a financial package that works for you? Create a checklist of your needs and priorities, and document how each of the colleges may or may not meet your expectations. This will give you a visual chart to help weigh your options.

6. Connect with a transfer advisor right away

Establishing a direct connection with the transfer advisor at each of the colleges you are considering is a key step in the transfer process. The transfer advisor will be an excellent resource and help guide you through the requirements for transfer, set up a campus visit, connect you with faculty in your desired program of study, provide you with a checklist of items to complete prior to transfer, and assist you in selecting current coursework that will apply toward the baccalaureate degree. You'll want to consult with them each term, prior to registration periods, to ensure that your courses are in line with your future degree requirements.

7. Evaluate how your credits will transfer

Most community colleges will have articulation agreements with select four-year colleges in their state or region. Articulation agreements are formally approved course plans or lists of individual courses that will be automatically accepted as equivalents to courses or requirements at the four-year college.

These agreements are typically provided by transfer advisors or may be published in the transfer section of the college website, and can serve as an excellent guide for course selection while attending the community college. This certainly does not mean that your credits won't transfer to four-year colleges that do not have an articulation agreement with your community college. Community college credit is commonly accepted at four-year colleges across the country. However, these agreements do help students to plan ahead and can pave the way for a smoother transfer of credits in many cases.

8. Build a timeline and track your progress toward transfer

Once you've narrowed down your choice of colleges, you'll want to establish a timeline and checklist to start working on all of the suggested items mentioned in this chapter. Keep your information organized and stored in one central location that you can refer to it on a regular basis during your community college journey. You'll want a separate file for each of the colleges you are considering. The file should contain contact information for the transfer advisor, information that you've collected for that college, a timeline and checklist of items that you'll need to complete, and any correspondence between you and the transfer college.

9. Make it a priority to transfer directly after graduation

Transferring on to the four-year college directly after completing a degree at the community college can increase the odds of successfully completing a baccalaureate degree within 6-years. According to a National Student Clearinghouse Research Center study, students who transferred to a four-year college within one year of community college graduation were 26% more likely to complete their bachelor's degree than students who stopped out for more than one year. It's not all that surprising, since most students who transfer right away are already in the learning mode and balancing the demands of life and college. So, it's best to keep moving toward your goal.

10. Start off as a successful transfer student

Once you've been accepted for admission and decided on the four-year college that's best for you, you'll have a new checklist of things to get working on. Don't forget to request an official final transcript to be sent to your four-year college. Common things you'll need to start doing right away to ensure a successful start as a transfer student:

- ✓ Complete the FAFSA with your transfer school listed to receive your SAR
- ✓ Ensure scholarship requirements are completed
- ✓ Attend a transfer orientation
- ✓ Sign on to the student portal to keep up with emails, financial aid info and more
- ✓ Meet with your new advisor
- ✓ Get registered for classes
- ✓ Make housing arrangements

Find More Tips and Strategies for Academic Success by Visiting: www.CollegeTransitionPublishing.com

Life During Community College Sources

Chapter 4 Campus Safety

Baum, Ph.D., Katrina, Shannon Catalano, Ph.D., Michael Rand, and Kristina Rose. "Stalking Victimization." USDOJ: Office on Violence Against Women. Web. 26 Oct. 2010. <http://www.ovw.usdoj.gov/>.

"College Drinking: A Snapshot of Annual High-Risk College Drinking Consequences." Research about Alcohol and College Drinking Prevention. National Institute of Alcohol Abuse and Alcoholism, 1 July 2010. Web. 31 Dec. 2010. <http://www.collegedrinkingprevention.gov/StatsSummaries/snapshot. aspx>.

Sampson, Rana. "Acquaintance Rape of College Students." COPS Community Oriented Policing Service. U.S. Department of Justice. Web. 28 June 2010. <http://www.cops.usdoj.gov/>.

"Seven Tips for Campus Safety." Security On Campus, Inc. Web. 01 Jan. 2011. <http://www.securityon-campus.org/index.php?option=com_content&view=article&id=1563>.

"The Campus Safety and Security Data Analysis Cutting Tool." Ope.ed.gov. U.S. Department of Education Office of Postsecondary Education, 2010. Web. 28 June 2010. <http://ope.ed.gov/security/>.

Chapter 5 Developing Relationships

Park, Kang H., and Peter M. Kerr. "Determinants of Academic Performance: A Multinomial Logit Approach." Journal of Economic Education Spring (1990): 101-11.

"Class Attendance." Minnesota State University Mankato. Web. 26 Oct. 2010. <http://www.mnsu.edu/cetl/teachingresources/articles/classattendance.html>.

Chapter 6 Academic Integrity

"Academic Honesty : Center for Academic Support." University of Rochester. 3 Sept. 2010. Web. 29 Dec. 2010. <http://www.rochester.edu/college/ccas/AdviserHandbook/AcadHonesty.html>.

Argetsinger, Amy. "Technology Exposes Cheating at U-Va." Washingtonpost.com. Web. 12 Sept. 2010. <http://www.washingtonpost.com/ac2/wp-dyn?pagename=article&node=&contentId=A638-2001May8>.

"Character Traits Associated with the Five Dimensions of Character and Social Responsibility." Association of American Colleges and Universities. Web. 29 Dec. 2010. <http://www.aacu.org/core_commitments>.

Definition of Plagiarism. "Glossary." The United States Department of Justice. Web. 29 Dec. 2010. <http://www.justice.gov/criminal/cybercrime/cyberethics_glossary.htm>.

Gabriel, Trip. "Plagiarism Lines Blur for Students in Digital Age." The New York Times 1 Aug. 2010, A1 sec. Web. 30 Sept. 2010. <www.nytimes.com>.

"Fundamental Values Project." Center for Academic Integrity. Web. 15 Sept. 2010. <http://www.academicintegrity.org/fundamental_values_project/>.

Chapter 7 Keys to Success

Bandura, A. "Self Efficacy." Encyclopedia of Human Behavior. Ed. V.S. Ramachaudran. 1994. Print.

Cloud, John. «Yes, I Suck: Self-Help Through Negative Thinking - TIME.» Www.time.com. Web. 11 Aug. 2010. <http://www.time.com/time/health/article/0,8599,1909019,00.html>.

Diversity of College Students: The Latest Research." DiversityWeb - A Resource Hub for Higher Education. Web. 02 Jan. 2011. <http://www.diversityweb.org/research_and_trends/research_evaluation_impact/benefits_of_diversity/impact_of_diversity.cfm>.

Payán, Rose M., and Michael T. Nettles. "Current State of English-Language Learners in the U.S. K-12 Student Popula-tion." ETS Home. Web. 5 Dec. 2010. <http://www.ets.org/>.

"Positive Attitude Delays Aging." BBC News - Home. Web. 02 Jan. 2011. <http://news.bbc.co.uk/2/hi/health/3642356.stm>.

Chapter 8 Health Insurance and Healthy Living

Davidson, Richard J., Jon Kabat-Zinn, Jessica Schumacher, Melissa Rosenkranz, Daniel Muller, Saki F. Santorelli, Ferris Urbanowski, Anne Harrington, Katherine Bonus, and John F. Sheridan. "Alterations in Brain and Immune Function Produced by Mindfulness Meditation." Psychosomatic Medicine 65.4 (2003): 564-70. Web.

Ramell, Wiveka, Philippe R. Goldin, Paula E. Carmona, and John R. Mcquaid. "The Effects of Mindfulness Meditation on Cognitive Processes and Affect in Patients with Past Depression." Cognitive Therapy and Research 28.4 (2004): 433-55. Web.

Federal Student Aid - Information on Grants, Student Loans, Scholarships and Other Financial Aid. Web. 1 Aug. 2010. <http://federalstudentaid.ed.gov/>.

"Funding Education Beyond High School 2010 - 2011." Student Aid on the Web. Web. 15 Aug. 2010. <http://studentaid.ed.gov/>.

College, Education, Financial Aid Info. Web. 21 Dec. 2013. <http://www.college.gov/>.

FAFSA on the Web-Federal Student Aid. Web. 21 Dec. 2013. <http://www.fafsa.ed.gov/>.

ACSM. Web. 02 Jan. 2011. <http://www.acsm.org/>.

Diagnostic and Statistical Manual of Mental Disorders: DSM-III-R. Washington, DC: American Psychiatric Association, 1994. Print.

Parker-Pope, Tara. "Gene Mutation Tied to Needing Less Sleep." The New York Times. 14 Aug. 2009. Web.

"What Happens When You Sleep?" National Sleep Foundation - Information on Sleep Health and Safety | Information on Sleep Health and Safety. Web. 24 Oct. 2010. <http://www.sleepfoundation.org/article/how-sleep-works/what-happens-when-you-sleep>.

http://journals.lww.com/psychosomaticmedicine/Abstract/2003/07000/Alterations_in_Brain_and_Immune_Function_Produced.14.aspx

Albert J. Arias, Karen Steinberg, Alok Banga, and Robert L. Trestman. The Journal of Alternative and Complementary Medicine. October 2006, 12(8): 817-832. doi:10.1089/acm.2006.12.817

Chapter 11 Homesickness

National Association of Insurance Commissioners (NAIC). Web. 1 Oct. 2010. <http://www.naic.org/>.

Chapter 15 Learning Styles

Coffey, Heather. "Experiential Education." LEARN NC. Web. 01 Sept. 2010. <http://www.learnnc.org/lp/pages/4967>.

"David A. Kolb on Experiential Learning." Contents @ the Informal Education Homepage. Web. 02 Jan. 2011. <http://www.infed.org/biblio/b-explrn.htm>.

Fisher, Alec. "Critical Thinking: An Introduction." Cambridge University Press, 2001. Web. 9 Sept. 2010. <http://catdir.loc.gov/catdir/samples/cam031/2002265188.pdf>.

Watson Glaser Critical Thinking Appraisal: WGCTA. --. Harcourt Brace World, 1964. Print.

Chapter 16 Memory Skills and Multitasking

Boyd, Robyrne. "Do People Only Use 10 Percent Of Their Brains?: Scientific American." Science News, Articles and In-formation | Scientific American. Web. 05 Oct. 2010. <http://www.scientificamerican.com/article.cfm?id=people-only-use-10-percent-of-brain>.

Chudler, Eric H. "Neuroscience For Kids - Explore the Nervous System." UW Faculty Web Server. Web. 02 Jan. 2011. <http://faculty.washington.edu/chudler/introb.html>.

"Does Multitasking Lead To A More Productive Brain? : NPR." NPR : National Public Radio : News & Analysis, World, US, Music & Arts : NPR. Web. 02 Aug. 2010. <http://www.npr.org/templates/story/story.php?storyId=127771658>.

Hallowell, Edward M. CrazyBusy: Overstretched, *Overbooked, and about to Snap : Strategies for Coping in a World Gone ADD.* New York: Ballantine, 2006. Print.

Merlo, Carol. "Too Much to Do and Not Enough Time: The Liability of Multi-Tasking." ArticlesBase.com. Web. 02 July 2010. <http://www.articlesbase.com/self-help-articles/too-much-to-do-and-not-enough-time-the-liability-of-multitasking-924021.html#ixzz0udU45pE4>.

"THE BRAIN FROM TOP TO BOTTOM." LE CERVEAU À TOUS LES NIVEAUX! Web. 02 Jan. 2011. <http://thebrain.mcgill.ca/flash/i/i_07/i_07_p/i_07_p_tra/i_07_p_tra.html>.

Chapter 18 Communication, Note Taking, and Study Skills

«Study Skills Resources.» Cornell Learning Strategies Center. Web. 02 Jan. 2011. <http://lsc.sas.cornell.edu/>.

"Toastmasters International - Visual Aids & PowerPoint." Toastmasters International - Home. Web. 02 Jan. 2011. <http://www.toastmasters.org/MainMenuCategories/FreeResources/NeedHelpGivingaSpeech/BusinessPresentations/VisualAidsPowerPoint.aspx>.

"Where To Study / How To Study." Dartmouth College. Web. 01 Aug. 2011. <http://www.dartmouth.edu/~acskills/success/study.html>.

Chapter 19 Test Taking Strategies

Greenberger, Dennis, and Christine A. Padesky. *Mind over Mood: Change How You Feel by Changing the Way You Think.* New York: Guilford, 1995. Print.

Chapter 21 Paying for College

«Checking Study: A Detailed Look at the Results.» Bankrate.com. Web. 02 Jan. 2011. <http://www.bankrate.com/brm/news/chk/chkstudy/20060417b2.asp>.

U.S. PIRG. Web. 02 Jan. 2011. <http://www.pirg.org/>.

Chapter 27 Planning

Shapiro, D., Dundar, A., Ziskin, M., Chiang, Y. Chen, J., Torres, V., & Harrell, A. (2013, August). Baccalaureate Attainment: A National View of the Postsecondary Outcomes of Students Who Transfer from Two-Year to Four-Year Institutions (Signature Report No. 5). Herndon, VA: National Student Clearinghouse Research Center.

Made in the USA
Columbia, SC
30 July 2017